MW00906035

ΛΛΛ AMERICAN **MARKETING** ASSOCIATION

AMA Handbook for
CUSTOMER
Satisfaction

ALAN DUTKA

**Published by NTC Business Books in Association with
the American Marketing Association**

AMERICAN
MARKETING
ASSOCIATION

NTC Business Books
NTC a division of *NTC Publishing Group* • Lincolnwood, Illinois USA

Library of Congress Cataloging-in-Publication Data

Dutka, Alan F.
    AMA handbook for customer satisfaction : research, planning, and
implementation / Alan Dutka.
        p.   cm.
    Includes bibliographical references and index.
    1. Consumers--Research.   2. Consumer satisfaction--Research.
I. Title.
HF5415.3.D88   1993
658.8'12--dc20   92-34249
                                                                    CIP

Published by NTC Business Books, a division of NTC Publishing Group
4255 West Touhy Avenue
Lincolnwood (Chicago), Illinois 60646-1975, U.S.A.
© 1994 by NTC Publishing Group. All rights reserved.
No part of this book may be reproduced, stored in a retrieval system,
or transmitted in any form or by any means,
electronic, mechanical, photocopying, recording, or otherwise,
without the prior permission of NTC Publishing Group.
Manufactured in the United States of America.

3 4 5 6 7 8 9 BC 9 8 7 6 5 4 3 2

Contents

Preface

C ustomer satisfaction is a growing concern to business organizations throughout the world. Consumers are becoming aggressive in demanding that products meet or exceed expectations. Outstanding product performance is required. The lowest prices consistent with excellent quality are also expected. Increased global competition is adding pressure to bottom-line profit performance and forcing companies to view their products and services from the customer's perspective.

Customer satisfaction is an integral part of total quality management. The customer drives total quality management by establishing expectations, standards, and performance requirements. Total quality management focuses on viewing products and services as solutions to customer problems.

Customer satisfaction research focuses on two key issues:

1. Understanding the expectations and requirements of the customer.

2. Determining how well a company and its major competitors are succeeding in satisfying these expectations and requirements.

Numerous books and articles have been written about the importance of understanding and satisfying customer requirements and expectations. Information about the step-by-step procedures needed to successfully implement customer satisfaction research, however, is very sparse. The objective of this book is to fill that void.

This book is a practical, step-by-step guide with outstanding work by academic researchers integrated throughout the text. The examples are based primarily on research conducted by the National Survey Research Center, a marketing and opinion research company located in Cleveland since 1949.

Illustrations include both business-to-business and consumer research. The applications range from satisfaction with a retail strip mall to industrial pipe manufacturers' satisfaction with suppliers of polyvinyl chloride resin. Names of companies have been changed, and some details have been modified to protect the confidentiality of the information. The illustrations, however, reflect real problems and real data. The open-ended responses found throughout the text are unedited comments taken from National Survey Research Center projects over the past few years.

Several leading business firms also contributed information and experiences to the book, among them Roadway Express, Burger King, SuperAmerica, Baxter Healthcare Corporation, and CalComp.

Because some of the technical topics touched on in this book would require separate texts to provide thorough explanations, some details have been omitted. Factor analysis, for example, is discussed without mentioning rotation strategies. A number of good references for further reading on these and other research topics are mentioned throughout the book.

The perceptual maps in Chapter 11 and Chapter 13 were generated using software developed by Market Action Research Software. Dr. Betsy Goodnow incorporated several proprietary algorithms and trade secrets in designing this software.

I extend a special thank you to staff members of the National Survey Research Center for the excellent comments and suggestions that they provided during various phases of the book's development. The efforts of David Kubic, Kelli Brigadoi, Lauren Wagner, Jeanette Hudak, Calvin Merchant, and Priscilla Dutka are sincerely appreciated. NTC Publishing Group exhibited high standards of professionalism toward every aspect related to the publication of this book. The efforts of Anne Knudsen, Karen Shaw, and Mary Englehart were especially appreciated.

1

Customer Satisfaction

The Challenge

ustomer satisfaction research is one of the fastest-growing segments of the marketing research industry. Satisfied customers offer businesses a promise of enhanced revenues and reduced operating costs. The promise must be pursued since recent trends in the business environment seem to have the opposite effect. Increased global competition, rising consumerism, and reduced profits have challenged the financial performance and priorities of U.S. corporations. Emphasis is shifting from cutting costs, reducing overhead, and eliminating employees, since many companies have already implemented such downsizing policies.

Foreign competition and deregulation are producing intense competitive pressures in many industries. The automobile indus-

---

Exhibit 1.1

Automobile Production: Percent Imports

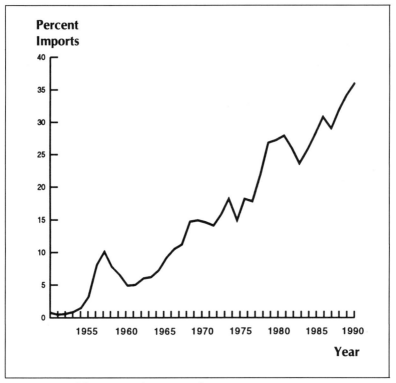

Source: Automobile News Market Data Book.

try, for example, has seen the percentage of foreign imports increase from less than 1 percent in the 1950s to more than 30 percent in the 1980s. The steady climb in imports is depicted graphically in Exhibit 1.1.

The success of the rebuilt Japanese industry received much attention in the 1980s and its impact on the United States has been dramatic. The percentage of Japanese television imports, for example, grew from zero in 1960 to more than 40 percent in 1986. This erosion of the U.S. market is shown in Exhibit 1.2. Similar trends exist in many other industries that once were the exclusive domain of the United States.

Consumers today are increasingly adamant about demand-

Exhibit 1.2

Television Production: Percent Imports

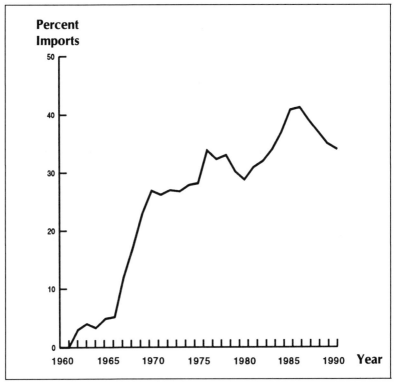

Source: Electronic Market Data Book.

ing quality products and services. The perception of the business community by the general public has also deteriorated significantly in the past few decades. These trends were reflected and amplified in the literature of the 1980s. Joseph Juran's success with Japanese industry was well publicized. Phil Crosby told American executives that "quality is free" and that costs are incurred only when requirements are not met. Peters and Waterman's *In Search of Excellence* gave new credibility to the "customer-focused" business orientation.

Initial customer satisfaction research indicated that both satisfied and dissatisfied customers dramatically affected a firm's bottom line. Here are three such findings:

■ One hundred satisfied customers generate 25 new customers.

■ For every complaint received, there are 20 other customers who feel the same way but do not bother to complain.

■ The cost of acquiring a new customer is five times as great as the cost of keeping a satisfied customer.

The numbers may differ by business or industry, but the message is obvious: Satisfied customers improve business and dissatisfied customers impair business.

Although satisfying customers may appear to be an elementary concept, serious research in this area is a new endeavor for many businesses. Very few businesses conduct the research in a rigorous manner, and an even smaller number of them effectively act on the results of the research.

Various approaches to determining customer satisfaction have been developed to meet differing requirements. While no methodology is perfect, principles and guidelines do exist to ensure that the research achieves the desired goals. The purpose of this book is to discuss and illustrate these methods by combining theory with realistic examples based on actual customer satisfaction studies.

The Malcolm Baldrige National Quality Award

In response to the widely recognized need for a national commitment to quality, the U.S. Department of Commerce in 1987 established the Malcolm Baldrige National Quality Award. The annual award recognizes U.S. companies that have excelled in quality achievement and quality management. It recognizes and encourages commitment to quality products and services.

The criteria used to judge companies serve as the blueprint for their self-evaluation. Seven major categories are included:

Percent Contribution	Category
30%	Customer satisfaction
15	Human resource utilization
15	Quality assurance
15	Quality results
10	Leadership
9	Strategic quality planning
6	Information and analysis

Note that customer satisfaction is by far the largest component of the award. This category is divided into eight subsections: knowledge of customer requirements and expectations, customer relationship management, customer service standards, commitment to customers, complaint resolution for quality improvement, customer satisfaction determination, customer satisfaction results, and customer satisfaction comparisons. These subsections are described in the Appendix. Research is a major factor in implementing all eight of them.

Winners of the prestigious Malcolm Baldrige Award are expected to use customer satisfaction research to:

■ Obtain a knowledge of customer requirements and expectations

■ Develop service standards

■ Measure satisfaction

■ Identify trends

■ Make comparisons with competition

They should also use the research indirectly to make cross-comparisons with other data, disseminate information throughout the organization, improve complaint resolution, and improve the company's commitment to its customers.

The awards are divided into three categories: large manufacturers, large service companies, and small businesses. In total, about fifty companies compete for the awards each year. Two awards are available in each category each year, but no more than five awards have actually been given in any year. The winners to date are:

1992	Large manufacturers:	American Telephone & Telegraph—Network Systems Operations
		Texas Instruments—Defense and Electronics Division
	Large service companies:	American Telephone & Telegraph—Universal Credit Card
		Ritz-Carlton Hotel Company
	Small businesses:	Granite Rock Co.
1991	Large manufacturers:	Solectron Corp.
		Zytec Corp.
	Large service companies:	none
	Small businesses:	Marlow Industries
1990	Large manufacturers:	Cadillac Motor Car Division
		IBM Rochester
	Large service companies:	Federal Express Corp.
	Small businesses:	Wallace Co. Inc.
1989	Large manufacturers:	Milliken & Company
		Xerox Business Products and Services
	Large service companies:	none
	Small businesses:	none

1988 Large manufacturers: Motorola, Inc.

                                  Commercial Nuclear Fuel—
                                  Division of Westinghouse
                                  Electric Corp.

      Large service companies: none

      Small businesses: Globe Metallurgical Inc.

The award winners vary greatly in terms of company size and type of business. Every winner, however, demonstrates a complete commitment to customer satisfaction, total quality management, continuous improvement, and total employee involvement. Globe Metallurgical Inc., for example, developed quality measuring improvements that reduced customer complaints by 91 percent. Westinghouse reports that 99.999 percent of the division's nuclear-fuel rod assemblies are flawless.

Excellent customer satisfaction research is a prerequisite for winning the Malcolm Baldrige Award. Outstanding research, however, is only one component of a quality process that must be integrated and coordinated throughout the organization. It should be recognized, moreover, that the establishment of the Malcolm Baldrige Award is simply an indicator of the importance of customer satisfaction. All companies, whether or not they compete for the award, should strive for improved customer satisfaction.

Focus on the Customer

Business success in today's competitive market requires that the seller adopt the customer's viewpoint. Sales of a product or service must satisfy the customer's objectives and requirements. Baxter Healthcare Corporation's commitment to customers, for example, includes this goal: "Reaching an objective understanding of our customers' requirements and using all our resources to satisfy those requirements." Baxter's customer policy sums up the need for customer satisfaction research: "The true measure of our success is decided by our customers."

The emphasis on the customer is evident at SuperAmerica, a subsidiary of Ashland Oil: "We don't want satisfied customers—we want delighted customers," proclaims John F. Pettus, president of SuperAmerica. Pettus says satisfying customers "is not window dressing. We live it." The benefits of this philosophy are obvious. SuperAmerica was named convenience store chain of the year by the trade publication *Convenience Store Decisions*.

Here is what some customers say about companies that have not adopted the viewpoint of focusing on the customer:

> They are not concerned about how our business is doing, so we go with the company that cares about us.

> They act like they have plenty of business and don't need ours. They certainly don't care about our goals or problems. But there are plenty of competitors who do care about us.

> They don't care. They think because they are so big that they will be around forever. With today's competition, they won't be.

> It's a factory. It has no warmth. You are treated just like a number on a computer. Other places are not like that, so that's where we go instead.

> I won't say that they lie, but you can't trust what they say. They used to care about customers, but those days are gone. They quit worrying about what the customer needs or requires.

> I was with them for 20 years but I dropped them. Once they got into computers, they didn't really care about anyone's individual needs.

> One of the salesmen told me he would get back to me with a price, but that was five years ago and I don't take them seriously anymore.

> They don't give a damn about our business, so I have forgotten about them.

> The district manager actually told me that he didn't care if I took my business elsewhere. He told me to kiss off.

These comments were extracted from recent consumer and business-to-business surveys. Each of the companies sponsoring the surveys was experiencing sales and financial problems when these customer comments were captured. One of the companies, the dominant market-share leader 20 years ago, was absorbed by a competitor in 1991.

Objectives of Customer Satisfaction Research

Customer satisfaction research must achieve these four major objectives:

1. Determine the critical performance attributes that result in customer satisfaction.
2. Assess performance of the company and its major competitors.
3. Establish priorities and take corrective action.
4. Monitor progress.

Customer satisfaction research has grown from a small, insignificant element to an important component of marketing research budgets. A great deal of progress has been made. Business, however, still has a long way to go to convince the public that customer satisfaction is a major corporate priority.

In a recent survey, for example, randomly selected adults were asked what customer satisfaction really meant to them. Although there were many positive comments, a large number of respondents were negative. Here are a few actual responses:

They are satisfied when they get in my wallet.

I always thought it was a line—a sales gimmick.

I hope it means that they have our interests at heart but I don't think so.

It's hard to say in this day and age—too much dishonesty.

They say they care what the customer thinks but I've never met a company that really does.

I haven't found any of those companies—the customer doesn't count.

Trying to build an image in the customer's mind but in reality it doesn't mean a blooming thing.

They are supposed to be looking out for the customer needs, but most of them are for their stockholders.

Nothing—companies are out for themselves, not customers.

Achieving the four objectives of customer satisfaction research listed above will reduce the number of negative comments. A truly customer-oriented company will convert negative perceptions to positive impressions. Even more significantly, the customer-focused company will prevent negative perceptions from occurring in the first place.

The challenge in researching customer satisfaction lies in recognizing that such research is only the first stage of an ongoing process of improving customer satisfaction. There must be a strong commitment on the part of the business firm to making the changes called for by the research. The pressures of competition necessitate a vigilance over customer satisfaction, and research in this area will provide the knowledge essential for competitive advantage.

2

Planning Customer Satisfaction Research

*I*ntelligent planning is an essential first step to ensure both the technical and the political success of customer satisfaction research. The results must generate actions that lead to improvement. The research must be technically correct to avoid providing misleading or inaccurate information that can culminate in poor decisions by management.

Implementing technically sound research does not guarantee that the results will be used. Improving customer satisfaction must involve the entire organization. The credibility of the process must be established by involving the firm in the initial stages. Discussions should be encouraged. Objections and concerns should be understood and confronted early in the process.

Internal Planning

Satisfied customers create increases in sales, revenues, and profits. Customers, however, do not become satisfied simply because a survey was taken. Surveys create expectations for improvement. Research impacting customer satisfaction must improve the sponsoring company's decision-making process. Organizations undertaking customer satisfaction research must be positioned to act decisively on the results.

Internal planning usually requires four to six weeks. The initial issues to address are not which research firm will conduct the research or whether a mail or telephone survey will be undertaken. The organization must first determine how the information will be used after it is collected and analyzed. It may be interesting for a company to learn that a competitor is experiencing problems meeting just-in-time delivery schedules. The critical issue, however, is how that knowledge will be incorporated in the development of the company's business strategies and plans.

The objectives, methods, results, and impact of the research must be communicated to employees and customers. Active involvement by employees in the planning stages will increase the understanding of the process, strengthen the acceptance of the research results, and inspire a commitment to improvement. Customers require feedback because a survey increases their expectations for improvement.

Internal planning should encompass these steps:

1. Determine who within the company will be involved in the planning phase.

2. Understand how the various levels of the organization will obtain and use the survey results.

3. Formulate a precise definition of customers.

4. Develop a list of customers and important subclassifications that will be used in the analysis phase.

5. Communicate the intent of the research to employees and major customers.

6. Involve the entire organization in the process; stimulate discussion; confront objections and issues.

Selecting a Marketing Research Company

If an outside research organization is to be used for the survey, three to five professional marketing research companies should be invited to submit proposals. The quality of the proposals will be enhanced if a comprehensive request for proposals is prepared. The request for proposal should contain sufficient detail to communicate the general scope and intent of the research.

The role of the marketing research company must be clearly defined, since the capabilities of such companies differ considerably. Some organizations with excellent data collection facilities, for example, are not as capable in analyzing data or generating recommendations. Research organizations should be given three to four weeks to respond to a request for proposal.

An individual or group must be selected to evaluate each of the research proposals. Criteria must be established to evaluate the proposals and select a supplier. The technical merits of the proposals are often evaluated independently of the cost proposals. This allows for a selection of potential suppliers on the merits of understanding the research problem and developing sound recommendations. An evaluation of the costs of the leading candidates can then be undertaken.

The factors to be considered in proposal evaluation can be grouped into three categories:

1. Technical
    a. Understanding of the requirements
    b. Compliance with the requirements
    c. Soundness of the approach
    d. Description of quality assurance procedures

2. Capability and experience
   a. Background and experience of the company
   b. Background and experience of the individuals directly assigned to the project
   c. Demonstration of past performance
   d. Soundness of the project plan, including time frame
   e. Nature and extent of any subcontracting

3. Cost
   a. Explanation of costs
   b. Comparison with other potential suppliers

The development of a request for proposal, the selection of potential suppliers, the submission of proposals, and the selection of a supplier will require six to eight weeks. A portion of this effort can be accomplished concurrently with internal planning.

Planning the Determination of Performance Attributes

The determination of the critical performance attributes (see Chapter 5) from the customers' perspective will consume about four to six weeks. The following tasks are involved:

1. Conduct interviews with employees.

2. Analyze indirect measures of customer satisfaction.

3. Conduct qualitative research with customers to determine preliminary requirements and expectations.

4. Conduct quantitative research with customers to solidify the requirements and expectations.

5. Analyze the results.

6. Present the results to the organization.

7. Finalize the critical performance attributes.

8. Obtain commitment from the employees.

An outside marketing research company may take responsibility for project planning at this stage. This phase of the research is critical and should not be rushed. Measuring and monitoring the performance factors that lead to satisfaction and dissatisfaction will generate the information essential for strategic and competitive planning. An inappropriate set of attributes will miss the mark.

Planning the Development and Implementation of the Survey

The company must remain actively involved in questionnaire development and survey implementation even if an outside marketing research organization is used. The tasks involved at this stage are:

1. Select the method for the survey (telephone, mail, etc.).
2. Formulate the generic questionnaire.
3. Expand the questionnaire by adding desired enhancements.
4. Determine the sample size.
5. Pretest the survey.
6. Train the interviewers.
7. Conduct the interviews.
8. Monitor quality control throughout the interviewing process.

A marketing research organization should be able to conduct at least 300 interviews per day. Conducting interviews, however, is only one aspect of implementation. Training, monitoring, scheduling callbacks, analyzing open-ended questions, developing conclusions and recommendations, and presenting results are also involved. All of these tasks are labor-intensive. A research organization should be allowed about four weeks to complete the job, with even more time allocated if the number of interviews exceeds 500 per day.

A time allowance of six months from initial planning to the development of recommendations is not uncommon:

Research Component	Number of Weeks
Internal planning	4–6
Selection of company	6–8
Definition of performance attributes	4–6
Conducting the survey	4–6
Analysis of survey results	1–2
Development of recommendations	1–2
Total	20–30

Each stage of customer satisfaction research is very important and should not be rushed. Presenting results, obtaining support from the organization, and implementing change will present a new set of challenges once the research has been completed.

3

Who Are the Customers?

*T*his chapter stresses the importance of customer identification in customer satisfaction research. Identifying customers through consumer research and business-to-business research, acquiring information about competitors' customers and internal customers, determining the methods to be used in selecting customers for research, and developing accurate definitions of customers—all help to establish the framework for successful customer satisfaction research.

Defining and identifying customers is a major challenge in customer satisfaction research. Consider the case of a prosperous regional company with over 50 retail outlets. Although the firm had been in business for 80 years, no records of its customers existed. When the company recently had need to determine its customers' satisfaction level, there was no customer identification data on which to base a study.

Another firm had a very sophisticated computerized database containing information about all past sales. Details at the individual customer level could be obtained about both the total number and the dollar amount of sales. History could also be obtained by individual product and by product group. Customers could be sorted and analyzed by geographic location, industry code, and company size. The name and telephone number of each purchaser was included.

The company, however, did not know the positions or titles of the purchasers. Customer satisfaction research indicated that the purchase decision makers ranged from summer college students to presidents of companies. Classification of purchasers into six major categories resulted in the following breakdown:

Percentage of Total Purchasers	Position Classification
39	Managers and supervisors
23	Executives and owners
19	Secretaries and administrative assistants
11	Purchasing agents
5	Engineers
3	Other professional positions

Perceptions of satisfaction differed considerably by position classification. Executives and owners, for example, tended to give the firm the lowest overall satisfaction ratings, and secretaries and administrative assistants were at the other extreme. Knowledge of the position or title of the purchaser was therefore critical in analyzing and interpreting the results of the customer satisfaction research and in developing strategies for improvement.

The importance of identifying customers is emphasized in the Malcolm Baldrige National Quality Award requirements:

Identify the market segments, customer and potential customer groups, including customers of competitors, and their requirements and expectations through surveys, interviews and other contacts.

Defining customers can be difficult even if a customer database exists. For example, who are the customers of a community college? Current students are certainly customers. College-bound youths are potential customers. Former students are past customers and could be potential customers. Parents of current or potential students may be influential in selecting a school and may be considered customers if they pay the tuition bill. Workers with specialized career-training requirements or adults desiring classes to improve their "quality of life" are potential customers. The businesses that hire the community college graduates may be considered customers. The community that supports the college by authorizing tax levies constitutes another type of customer.

A public utility has both residential and business customers. A nursing home must satisfy the expectations of both the residents and the family members who directly or indirectly influence decisions on the residents' care. Both the public utility and the nursing home must also fulfill the requirements of government regulatory agencies—another type of customer whose satisfaction is critical.

The opinions of customers of competitors are obviously important. Customer satisfaction research also includes internal customers. Every employer has internal customers within the company. The payroll department, for example, services the entire organization. Internal satisfaction influences relationships with external customers.

It is apparent, then, that the comprehensive and accurate identification of customers is critical to the success of any customer satisfaction study.

Identifying Customers

Consumer Research

Identifying past, current, and potential customers can be a difficult process. For example, is a customer who made regular monthly purchases for five years and then stopped for the past three months a current or past customer? Is the purchaser of a long-lasting durable good, such as a refrigerator, a current customer even if a new purchase has not been made in the past five years?

The purchaser and the user of a product may also differ. Who, for example, is the "customer" when an adult purchases breakfast cereal to be consumed by a 6-year-old child? Family-oriented products, such as automobile and home entertainment centers, may involve many users with different viewpoints regarding expected performance.

A potential customer is sometimes characterized as an individual with a need or desire for a product, a motivation to buy, the necessary cash or credit, and an available store or other outlet to conduct the purchase. This description is difficult to apply to a "customer" of a metropolitan park system when potential customers are considered voters who will support the park system when the next levy renewal is submitted for approval. These customers may never have used the product. Conversely, a regular user of the park system who is not a registered voter is not considered a customer.

For many businesses, list or computer files of customers may not exist. This is especially true for retail, grocery, and department stores. Files of charge account customers are often helpful. These customers, however, may not be representative of the businesses's total customer base. Ignoring customers who pay in cash may introduce a serious bias in the customer satisfaction survey results.

Preliminary research, sometimes of a creative nature, may be required to adequately identify a company's customers. For example, many retail booksellers offer discounts to "club members." The discount program generates a list of customers not otherwise available.

There are no standard answers to the questions raised in this section. Each company must make appropriate definitions and decisions to designate the individuals who will qualify as customers. The critical point is to raise and properly address the numerous questions involved in adequately defining customers.

Business-to-Business Research

Identifying customers in business-to-business research is also difficult. The decision maker may differ from the ultimate user of a product or service. Executive management, for example, will often have different requirements and expectations from those of technical users. Corporate offices may have a different view of satisfaction than that of branch plants or operational units. Executive management and corporate offices, however, may make the purchase decisions. Research geared to the wrong individuals may result in the development of strategic and action plans that are doomed to failure.

Channels of distributions also complicate the definition of a customer. Dealers and other intermediaries influence how a product or service is perceived by the actual consumer. Questions about these intermediaries should be included in a satisfaction survey directed to the ultimate consumer. Moreover, dealers and distributors should be interviewed to determine how they view training, product education, pricing, sales support, and the product characteristics important to the ultimate consumer.

Once again, there is no universal formula to define customers. The company conducting satisfaction research must understand who the decision makers are within the customer's organizational structure. Identification of individuals within each company who influence these decision makers is also critically important. The individuals who influence and make the decisions about the products or services in question are the best candidates for customer satisfaction research. Identification of these individuals, either by name or title, may require preliminary research.

Customers Of Competitors

Accurate information about competitors is always valuable, but it is often difficult to obtain. A customer satisfaction survey is an excellent vehicle for gaining competitive intelligence.

A few customers will refuse to provide information about competitors. The overwhelming majority of customers, however, will be willing to share perceptions and insights about competitors' strengths and weaknesses. Talking with former customers also provides an opportunity to determine both the sources of dissatisfaction and the strengths of competitors.

Internal Customers

Many companies include internal customers in their customer satisfaction research. Every employee in an organization is a customer of other individuals within the company. The payroll, accounting, management information services, human resources, and legal departments have internal customers with requirements and expectations.

Considering internal customers is not frivolous, for customer satisfaction requires total company involvement. Direct parallels exist between how employees treat each other and how they treat customers. Employee satisfaction influences customer satisfaction. An internal "quality" atmosphere creates an environment conducive to satisfying external customers. A company that meets its employees' requirements is in an ideal position to satisfy its external customers' requirements.

Some organizations institute internal quality awards to departments or individuals who exemplify a commitment to customer satisfaction. This practice encourages and cultivates the quality atmosphere necessary to achieve customer satisfaction.

Customer satisfaction research relating to internal customers should parallel research relating to external customers. Once requirements, expectations, and performance attributes are established, progress is monitored over time.

Methodology for Selecting Customers for Research

The methodology used to select customers for satisfaction research is very important. The technical aspects associated with correctly selecting a sample of customers are complex. The reasons why a properly developed methodology is important are discussed in this section. Mathematical details, however, are omitted.

Well developed methodologies exist to make inferences about an entire population of customers based on results obtained from a sample of these customers. The mathematical theory is based on the concept of randomness. In this context, randomness means that every customer in the population has an equal and independent chance of being selected in the sample.

Random sampling is often illustrated by drawing chips from a thoroughly mixed bowl. Even this highly idealistic illustration is very difficult to implement practically. The true randomness of military draft lotteries during the Vietnam war, for example, has been subject to considerable technical debate.

Suppose that a computer database contains information about every customer of a company. Some of the customer information, unfortunately, is duplicated. A sample is drawn and duplicate customer information is deleted from the sample. The sample is not random since certain customers had a greater chance of being selected. To achieve randomness, the duplicated customers should have been deleted from the computer database, not the resulting sample.

Consider customer satisfaction research designed to measure parents' satisfaction with a local school district. An important demographic statistic is whether or not the parents own their own home (since tax levies are assessed against homeowners). A random sample of school children is selected and the proportion of families who own homes is computed from the survey results. A bias arises because a family with four children has four times the chance of being represented in the sample as families with one child. Large families are over-represented and smaller families are under-represented.

The families, rather than the children, should be randomly selected. A random sample of children can produce unbiased results if the responses are properly weighted. Each response should be divided by the total number of children in the family.

Even if complete randomness is achievable, it may not be the best sampling strategy. For example, stratified sampling, which guarantees representation among different sizes of customer accounts, may be desirable. Quota sampling, where demographic groups are represented in the same proportion as the overall population, is also commonly implemented. Each of these strategies has both strengths and weaknesses, and different methods of mathematical analysis.

Mathematical details are not the only reason for implementing a carefully developed sampling plan. One firm, for example, generated three lists of customers based on purchase quantity: small, medium, and large. One customer appeared on all three lists. Although the error was corrected prior to interviewing, the potential existed for calling the same customer three times in one day to inquire about satisfaction. Survey bias was reduced with the elimination of the redundant information. Reducing the possibility of irritating the customer was also important. References that discuss the development of technically correct sampling plans include Henry, Deming, and Kish.

Action Plan for Determining Customers for Research

In customer satisfaction research, precise definitions of customers are essential. These definitions may be modified as the research proceeds, but problems or difficulties must be resolved early in the research planning. To this end, the following steps must be taken in the preliminary stage of the research process:

1. Formulate precise definitions of the customers to be surveyed.

2. Develop categories of customers who might logically participate in satisfaction research: current customers, past customers, potential customers, or some combination of these categories.

3. Develop a list or computer file of customers.

4. Review the list for accuracy and completeness.

5. Determine if a sample is required or if every customer is to be interviewed.

6. Devise a sampling methodology for selecting customers from the file.

7. Establish subcategories for which information is vital: customer size, account size, geographic area, type of industry, and the like.

8. Screen the final list for possible duplication.

4

Qualitative and Quantitative Research

*C*ustomer satisfaction research methodologies can be divided into qualitative and quantitative categories. *Qualitative research* involves free-format responses in which words and observations are used. It provides in-depth information obtained from a few cases. The results are used as exploratory research. The small number of cases, however, cannot establish statistically reliable information for generalizations to a larger population. Two specific qualitative methodologies are in-depth interviews and focus groups. These techniques are discussed in the next two sections.

Quantitative research concentrates on numbers to represent viewpoints and opinions. The information is usually obtained from telephone or mail questionnaires. The numbers, generated from a larger number of cases, are manipulated using arithmetic and statistics. Quantitative techniques are discussed in depth in Chapters 10 and 11.

Choosing qualitative or quantitative research is not an either-or situation. The methodologies are complementary and should be combined to maximize their individual strengths. Initial qualitative research, for example, can be used to help develop an effective quantitative telephone or mail questionnaire. Qualitative research can also be used after a telephone or mail survey to explain or provide additional insight into unanticipated results in the quantitative survey.

Some of the major differences between qualitative and quantitative research are summarized in the following table:

	Qualitative	Quantitative
Type of research	Exploratory	Descriptive/ statistical
Type of question	Open-ended (probing)	Closed-ended
Number of respondents	Small	Large
Analysis	Subjective	Statistical
Interviewer qualifications	Special skills required	Less need for special skills
Generalization of results	Very limited	Reasonable

Qualitative Research

In-Depth Interviews

In-depth interviews are face-to-face interviews conducted on a one-on-one basis or in very small groups. These interviews resemble conversations more than formal, structured interviews.

A detailed discussion outline must be designed prior to conducting the interviews. Questions should be general and nondirective. That is, the questions must not direct a response toward fixed, predetermined choices but instead allow the respondent to state whatever thoughts occur. The questions are asked in a relaxed, casual manner. Time must be taken to explore and investigate important ideas.

In-depth interviews are especially appropriate for capturing the ideas and viewpoints of key executives within an organization—the sponsoring company or one of the major customers in business-to-business research. Excellent insights can also be obtained from customer-service representatives within the sponsoring company.

The interviewer must allow a free flow of ideas while still controlling the interview by providing the necessary order and structure. Important ideas and concepts must be recognized and probed for additional information.

A probe is a neutral remark that prompts the respondent to clarify or elaborate on a previous statement. Certain words usually indicate the need for a probe. Examples include *quality*, *good*, *convenient*, *service*, and *reputation*. The probe should never lead the respondent into an answer. For example, a statement like "Don't you think that . . ." will certainly bias the survey results.

Probes can take many forms:

1. Pausing expectantly—looking intently at the respondent with an expectation that he or she will continue the discussion

2. Repeating the last part of the respondent's statement as a question: "Service is the most important requirement?"

3. Asking a question:

    "Could you give me an example of that?"
    "Could you tell me more about that?"
    "In what way?"
    "How do you mean that?"
    "What causes you to feel that way?"

Questions used as probes should be standardized so that uniformity is achieved among different interviewers.

A tape recorder should be used during the interviews. A transcription can then be generated by an individual skilled at this task. The use of a tape recorder reduces the almost unavoidable bias created by an interviewer documenting his or her own work.

Focus Groups

Focus groups are composed of seven to twelve persons who share common characteristics. The groups meet for about two hours to offer opinions, viewpoints, and perceptions about a predetermined topic (e.g., customer requirements and expectations).

Focus group sessions generate information that is not easily obtainable using other methods. Interactions among the group members often stimulate thinking in a manner not possible with other interviewing techniques.

Both consumer and business decisions are often influenced by emotion. A former customer, for example, discussing why he switched to a competitor, explained: "It was impulsive. It was not one particular reason but little, insignificant stuff. I decided to let a competitor have a crack at it and they haven't given us any reason to switch back." Viewpoints of this nature are easier to discover in a focus group environment than in a more structured telephone interview or in a mail questionnaire.

Focus groups composed of a company's customers are essential to the development of customer expectations and requirements. Three components are important to the success of a focus group:

1. Recruitment of the correct participants

2. Quality of the questions

3. Skills of the moderator

The basis and methodology for recruiting focus group participants must be discussed and agreed upon. Some market research organizations, for example, recycle participants from previous focus groups. Although this practice reduces the cost of recruiting participants, the participants cannot be considered random selections since they have been introduced and conditioned to the focus group environment.

An experienced focus group participant could be viewed as a consultant who is being used to help develop later quantitative research. This viewpoint might be justified because the focus group results should never, in any case, be directly generalized to a larger population. Most researchers, however, believe that "professional" focus group participants are not representative of any target population. The merits of these viewpoints should be debated and understood prior to recruiting focus group participants.

To guide the focus group session, a sequence of questions, often called a discussion outline, is developed in advance. The sample outline in Exhibit 4.1 is concerned with how business customers select vendors for office supply products. A two-hour session covering the following five major topics is planned:

1. How do customers choose office supply product vendors?

2. What is the definition and importance of quality?

3. How important is ordering assistance?

4. How do product guarantees impact the selection of a supplier?

5. What are customer perceptions about catalogs?

The discussion outline is not a questionnaire. All of the 33 questions could not possibly be asked during one two-hour session. Information relating to many of the questions will be volunteered during the normal course of the discussion without any prompting by the moderator. The moderator uses the outline to ensure that the relevant topics are covered in sufficient depth, to offer well-prepared questions for discussion, and to keep the session on track in terms of both content and time.

The moderator must be experienced at responding to unexpected or unanticipated opinions. For example, one company, feeling confident about the value and acceptance of a new product, conducted a focus group to help determine the initial price for the product. The focus group participants provided some unexpected responses, shown on page 32.

Exhibit 4.1

Focus Group Discussion Outline: Purchase of Office Supply Products

1. Selection of Vendor for Office Supply Products
- Thinking back to the last time you purchased an office supply product, how did you select the supplier?
- What are some words that describe an ideal supplier?
- What are the important factors that you consider when choosing a vendor for office supply products?
- Where do you usually purchase office supply products (catalog, office supply store, discount store)? What factors influence that choice?
- What are your experiences with these different methods of purchasing office supply products?
- Is it better to purchase certain products from one source rather than another? What are some examples?
- How do you feel about premiums or gifts being offered when you purchase office supplies?
- What do you think of the "one-stop-shopping" concept for buying office supply products?
- How often do you evaluate different suppliers for office supply products?

2. Quality
- Tell us about differences in quality that you have observed among the various types of suppliers.
- Describe some problems that you have experienced because of poor-quality office supply products.
- How do you define quality related to office supply products?
- How important is quality in your purchase decisions?
- Are there office supply products where quality is not very important? Where it is critically important?

- Are there products where it is possible to have too high quality—products where you are not willing to pay a higher price for top quality?
- What companies offer the best quality? The poorest quality?
- How do you feel about the statement "You get what you pay for" in relation to office supply products? Can you describe a situation in which this statement was not true?

3. **Assistance in Ordering**
   - Describe a situation in which assistance in ordering was very important when obtaining an office supply product.
   - How do you feel about the importance of assistance when you order office supplies?
   - Tell us about a time when you experienced problems obtaining assistance.
   - What companies offer the best ordering assistance? The poorest?

4. **Product Warranty**
   - What is your experience with product warranties associated with office supply products?
   - What difficulties have you experienced with product warranties? What "success stories" have you encountered?
   - How important is the product warranty in choosing a supplier?
   - What makes a good warranty?
   - What companies offer the best warranty?

5. **Catalogs**
   - What companies send you catalogs for office supply products?
   - What are your impressions of office supply catalogs?
   - Describe a situation where a catalog was a big help in making a purchasing decision.
   - What makes a good catalog?
   - How could the catalogs be improved?
   - Do you usually keep the catalogs? For how long?
   - How often would you like to receive a catalog from a supplier?

The product is a rip-off. I wouldn't pay anything for it.

Do they think we are a bunch of jerks?

Why would anyone pay for that?

This development was an example of failure to understand a product's appeal from the customer's perspective. The moderator in this case abandoned the predetermined outline and shifted from questions about price to a discussion of why the product was viewed negatively.

The number of participants and the length of the focus group meeting are somewhat arbitrary. Sessions with less than six participants may not produce the anticipated diversity of opinion and breadth of group discussion. Opportunities for individual participation may be limited when the group exceeds twelve members. Distracting side discussions often result when the group is too large. Meetings lasting longer than two hours can foster fatigue and loss of interest.

There are a number of marketing research firms specializing in customer satisfaction research, and these usually have qualitative research capabilities. The background and experience of the moderator is very important in choosing a research firm. A male moderator, one who might, for example, be very successful with industrial assignments, may not be the best choice to moderate a session composed of teenage girls. Other factors influencing the choice of research service firms include participant recruitment practices, analysis and management reporting capabilities, the physical environment in which the sessions will be conducted, and, of course, the cost of the services.

Discussion Guides for Focus Groups

In customer satisfaction research, making lists of customer requirements and expectations may provide some valuable insights. Customers, however, usually do not think about satisfaction in terms of a checklist of requirements. A spirited, energetic conversation will be more productive. A moderator, for example, might introduce such questions as:

- What is it like doing business with the _____ Company?

- If you were talking to the president of the _____ Company, what would you tell him or her about the company's product?

- Describe a time when you were very satisfied with the company's product or service.

- What were some of the circumstances when you were very dissatisfied with the product or service?

- What action did the company take to rectify your problem?

- What do you expect from a superior company in this industry?

- What would you tell a friend or relative about the _____ Company?

- What are some of the factors that have allowed your company to keep that account for so long?

- What were the circumstances that caused your company to lose that account?

- How would you compare Company _____ to Company _____?

The moderator should not ask direct questions about good or bad service. Instead, the moderator should determine what service means to customers and how competitors differ in providing service. The responses should be probed to determine customer expectations and requirements.

Transcripts of focus group discussions provide valuable input to some very sophisticated techniques for analyzing qualitative data. These techniques are discussed in Chapter 9.

The literature on qualitative research and focus groups is extensive. Bogdan and Taylor, for example, provide a good introduction to qualitative research, and Krueger presents an excellent overview of focus group research.[1]

---

[1]Complete bibliographical information for all literature references is given in the Bibliography at the back of this book.

Quantitative Research

Quantitative research is used to develop statistically reliable information from sample data that can be generalized to a larger population. This research usually involves surveys that are conducted by mail or telephone.

A major objective of this type of research is to quantify the information generated in the qualitative research phase. For example, focus group participants may indicate that the warranty is an important factor in choosing among competing products. Quantitative research is then used to establish the validity of this preliminary conclusion and to further identify the customers' expectation:

> How important is a warranty to your purchase decision: very important, somewhat important, not too important, or not at all important?

> In your opinion, what time period should the warranty cover?

Quantitative research is used to develop specific objectives, goals, and performance standards based on customer expectations. For example, the question:

> What length of time for product delivery would you consider achievable by an outstanding company?

will enable a company to change the performance standard:

> We will deliver all products as quickly as possible.

to include a measurable performance criterion that is important to the customer:

> Our company will deliver all products within two days of purchase.

Quantitative research is also a key factor in developing and implementing satisfaction measurements that are tracked and compared over time.

The advantages and disadvantages of the various types of survey research are summarized in Exhibit 4.2. The strengths and weaknesses of the methodologies can be used in determining the extent of qualitative and quantitative research required.

Exhibit 4.2

Advantages and Disadvantages of Various Research Methodologies

IN-DEPTH PERSONAL INTERVIEWS

Advantages:
- Complex questions can be explored.
- More in-depth responses are obtained.
- Responses that might be viewed negatively by a group are easier to obtain.
- A longer interview can be conducted (as compared with a telephone interview).
- Use of visual aids is very effective.

Disadvantages:
- Cost is greater than with other methodologies.
- Time to completion is longer than for telephone interviews.
- Number of completed interviews is smaller than with mail and telephone interviews.

FOCUS GROUPS

Advantages:
- Complex questions can be explored.
- More in-depth responses are obtained.
- Group interactions generate information that is not otherwise obtainable.
- An excellent method for generating ideas for a mail or telephone survey or for further in-depth analysis of results from a mail or telephone survey.

Disadvantages:
- Results cannot be generalized to a larger population.
- Information is almost always qualitative rather than quantitative.

continued

TELEPHONE SURVEYS

Advantages:
- Interviewing can be monitored and supervised, thus providing the best method for quality control.
- Response rate is much greater than with mail surveys, thus reducing bias associated with nonresponse.
- Time to complete the project is shorter than with either mail surveys or personal interviews.
- Cost is lower than with personal interviews and may not be greater than with mail surveys.

Disadvantages:
- Cost may be higher than with mail surveys (depending on response rates).
- Some respondents may be difficult to reach by telephone (irregular work hours, not at home, no telephone, etc.)
- Telephone interviews often generate quick responses, allowing inadequate time for in-depth thinking.

MAIL SURVEYS

Advantages:
- Cost is sometimes lower per completed interview (depending on response rate).
- Respondents are under no pressure to provide quick answers.

Disadvantages:
- Quality control is difficult or impossible (questions can be skipped, open-ended responses are not probed, etc.).
- Response rate is generally much poorer than with other methodologies.
- Bias due to nonresponse is much greater than with telephone surveys.
- Information from open-ended questions can be negligible and incomplete, since probing by interviewers is not possible.
- Respondents must have a reasonable proficiency in writing to give open-ended responses.

5

Determining Critical Performance Attributes

The Customer Defines Satisfaction

C ustomer satisfaction research is concerned with determining the extent to which products and services meet customers' wants and needs. These wants and needs create expectations. Meeting customer expectations results in satisfaction and exceeding expectations may create strong customer loyalty. Conversely, not meeting expectations results in dissatisfaction.

Requirements and expectations are formalized in a set of performance attributes. These attributes capture the important issues about how customers judge a product or company. Attributes will differ by company and industry.

Performance attributes are a central component of all three major phases of customer satisfaction research:

Phase 1: Determining the performance attributes that generate satisfied and dissatisfied customers.

Phase 2: Measuring satisfaction for an initial period to serve as a reference point for future surveys.

Phase 3: Conducting ongoing research to monitor progress.

Phase 1 activities are discussed in this chapter. The performance attributes that generate satisfied and dissatisfied customers are developed using two major guidelines:

1. The performance attributes must be important to the customer. An attribute involving "innovative, state-of-the-art technology and problem solutions" may be an ego builder for the company sponsoring the research but of very little importance to the customer. The only way to guarantee the selection of attributes that customers consider critical is to get the customers' opinions.

2. The performance attributes must be under the control and influence of the company. Customer satisfaction surveys create expectations that improvement is imminent. Time and effort should not be spent on areas that cannot or will not be changed by company actions.

The research must reveal not only the degree of customer satisfaction but also the underlying causes of satisfaction and dissatisfaction. This is accomplished by formulating performance attributes that are defined by the customer and under the control of the company.

Critical performance attributes are determined through a

combination of qualitative and quantitative research techniques, including in-depth interviews, focus groups, mail surveys, and telephone interviews.

Developing Preliminary Performance Attributes

Company knowledge is the first source of information about critical performance attributes. Executives know their business and their customers. Interviews with executives, sales representatives, and customer service personnel are important both to obtain information and to encourage involvement in the research process.

Customer satisfaction must then extend beyond the company and into the arena of the customer, particularly when requirements and expectations are to be defined. Satisfaction research must be viewed from the customer's perspective. There is no substitute for communicating directly with the customer. Here is a sample of perceptions that could be generated only by actually talking to customers:

> Maybe I expect too much from them, but on the other hand, they have never gone out of their way to find out what I expect.

> The sales rep's name is Robert Huff—whoever he is. I have never seen him. If he walked through the front door, I wouldn't know him from Adam.

> They are very rude. If I had the money, I would buy the company just so I could have the satisfaction of firing the staff in Los Angeles.

> I honestly believe that they have the worst sales reps in the business and I feel the company must make them this way. They come in complaining of long hours and having to hide in the rest rooms.

Exploratory qualitative research is the first step in defining critical performance attributes. In-depth interviews and focus groups involving company executives, employees who deal directly with customers, current and former customers, sales representatives, and suppliers provide a framework for identifying and understanding the important performance attributes.

The final set of performance attributes is selected with the help of a mail or telephone survey of customers. Customers rate the preliminary performance attributes on a scale of importance (i.e., 5 = very important to 1 = not at all important).

Surveys used to develop performance attributes are generally longer than surveys used to measure satisfaction. Unfortunately, customers may object to long, detailed telephone interviews. An alternative is to have the interviewer conduct a short telephone survey and then ask for further cooperation by completing a detailed mail survey. Or fax technology can be put to use. A short telephone interview can be followed with a fax document that includes more detail. The fax should be sent to the respondent immediately, with a request to return the completed questionnaire by fax. This procedure promotes a sense of urgency and is very likely to increase the response rate when compared with a mail survey.

Selecting performance attributes entirely on the basis of the highest average scores is usually a poor strategy. Similar attributes will be highly correlated. Several different versions of one important theme are likely to appear among the highest-rated attributes. The final survey should contain only one of these versions.

Several statistical techniques can be used to help select the final set of attributes. For example, factor analysis divides the survey data into underlying "dimensions." One attribute can be selected from each dimension, with the statistical results providing guidance in the selection.

Another statistical technique, discriminant analysis, is used to determine if the selected performance attributes are good predictors of overall satisfaction and dissatisfaction. Several iterations of factor analysis and discriminate analysis will generate a set of performance attributes that is both statistically valid and logically suitable for measuring customer satisfaction. These statistical techniques are discussed in Chapter 11.

Statistical analyses are very important in guiding the final selection of performance attributes. Management may also include specific attributes, regardless of statistical significance, to formulate strategic marketing plans.

Universal Performance Attributes

The performance attributes listed below are universally recognized and apply to many different products and services:

> *Attributes related to the product:*
> Value–price relationship
> Product quality
> Product benefits
> Product features
> Product design
> Product reliability and consistency
> Range of products or services
>
> *Attributes related to service:*
> Guarantee or warranty
> Delivery
> Complaint handling
> Resolution of problems
>
> *Attributes related to purchase:*
> Courtesy
> Communication
> Ease or convenience of acquisition
> Company reputation
> Company competence

These performance attributes are candidates for inclusion in almost all customer satisfaction surveys. However, they need to be further defined, clarified, and interpreted for each application.

Business-Specific Performance Attributes

Some performance attributes are specific to certain businesses and services. Examples of such attributes are given in Table 5.1.

Table 5.1

Performance Attributes for Specific Businesses and Services

Business/Service	Performance Attribute
Financial institution	Prompt replacement of lost credit cards Automatic teller machines operating without downtime
Computer dealer	Availability of replacement parts Response time for repairs
Restaurant	Cleanliness of tables, glasses, silverware
Furniture store	Delivery policy
Automobile manufacturer	Reliable starting in adverse environmental conditions Traction on ice and snow
Long-distance telephone carrier	Quality of transmission
Health care provider	Explanation of treatment options
Pizzeria	30-minute delivery
Trucking company	Pickup in 4 hours

Customer satisfaction research must also capture performance attributes specific to the individual organization. These attributes are the unique aspects of the organization and its culture that differentiate it from its competitors. International Business Machines (IBM), for example, has developed a reputation for excellent service, while McDonald's is noted for product consistency and cleanliness.

The following case studies illustrate the definition of performance attributes at various stages of the research process.

C A S E   S T U D Y

Satisfaction with an Energy Utility Company
Developing Preliminary Performance Attributes
Based on Executive Interviews

Developing performance attributes for customers of an energy utility is not as straightforward as it may appear. Performance attributes, for example, will differ between residential and business customers. A great deal of variability may exist even within each of these two broad groups. Home owners, for example, are more interested than renters in billing procedures and rate structures.

The attribute concepts in Exhibit 5.1 were formulated during a very preliminary stage of performance attribute development for residential customers. Company executives had been interviewed, but customers of the utility had not yet provided input into the process. The next step was to conduct focus groups comprised of home owners. The objectives of the focus groups were to (1) discuss the service and satisfaction issues that are important to the customer, and (2) discover ideas that are not represented in the preliminary list of performance attributes.

The focus group discussions revealed that many customers felt that advertising was not appropriate because of the monopoly status of utilities. Customers appeared unaware of the intense competitive pressures among alternative energy sources. This input was important both in developing the customer satisfaction survey and in creating a new advertising message.

The relevant attributes in Exhibit 5.1 and the input from the focus groups were then transformed into a second list of preliminary performance attributes. Next, a telephone survey was conducted to quantify the importance of these attributes from the customers' perspective. The survey determined, for example, that accurate billing and quick response for emergency service were very important to customers. Information and advertising included with the bill was viewed as much less important.

The results from the telephone survey, which indicated areas of both strength and weakness, were used to develop the final set of performance attributes. These were the attributes used in the customer satisfaction survey.

Since customers' views of utilities change relatively slowly, the survey is repeated on an annual basis rather than quarterly.

Exhibit 5.1

Preliminary Performance Attributes: Residential Customers of a Utility Company

Overall Service
Service quality
Service reliability
Responsiveness to routine service calls
Responsiveness to emergency service calls
Resolution of service problems

Price/Rates
Fairness of price
Good value indicated by price
Company concern about rates
Operating efficiencies implemented to offset rate increases

Billing
Accuracy of billing
Clarity of billing
Method of payment
Resolution of billing problems

Advertising
Advertising message recall
Advertising media recall
Advertising believability
Usefulness of the message

Interaction with Customers
Assistance provided to customers
Responsiveness to questions and inquiries
Courteousness of employees

Community Involvement
Assistance in making the community a better place to live
Provision of resources to help solve community problems

Social Responsibility
  Concern for customer safety
  Concern for environmental impact
  Actions to ensure future energy supplies
  Helping customers who cannot pay their bills

Competitive Evaluation
  Other companies in same field
  Gas, electric, and telephone company comparisons

C A S E   S T U D Y

Satisfaction with an Insurance Company
Developing Preliminary Performance Attributes Based on In-Depth Interviews

An insurance company was interested in determining the performance attributes that were important to current and potential policy holders. The development of performance attributes in this application was very challenging. The product is intangible until a claim is submitted. The monetary value of the product, therefore, is deferred to the future. The sale of the product often results in a long-term relationship in which the sale marks the beginning rather than the end of an association.

In-depth interviews with insurance agents uncovered an interesting perspective relevant to defining the performance attributes. The agents delineated two distinctly different groups that must be satisfied: the group of consumers who purchase the insurance and the insurance company that issues the policies.

The expectations of these two groups can be in direct conflict. A consumer, for example, may wish to obtain automobile insurance for an 18-year-old son. The company evaluates its agents on their ability to generate new business. A conflicting objective, however, is to obtain automobile insurance business that will lower the agents' ratios of claims to sales. Insuring an 18-year-old male will not be viewed as helping to meet that objective.

Table 5.2 presents the list of preliminary performance attributes generated from the perspective of the agents.

Table 5.2

Preliminary Performance Attributes:
An Insurance Company

Purchaser's Expectations

Thorough knowledge of the insurance business
Ability to clearly describe features of the policy
Ability to recommend sensible alternatives
Follow-through to get the policy issued quickly
Avoidance of high-pressure sales tactics
Availability when problems arise

Insurance Company Expectations

Dollar value of new business
Quality of sales (claims-to-sales ratio)
Use of centralized computer systems (word processing,
    spreadsheets, claim information, applications)
Knowledge of existing products
Knowledge of new products
Progress toward obtaining CLU (Chartered Life Underwriter) and
    CPCU (Chartered Property and Casualty Underwriter) status

---

Obtaining the customers' viewpoints was the next step in defining the critical performance attributes for insurance agents. A series of focus group discussions with consumers, for example, was undertaken. The discussions had the following objectives: to help validate the opinions of the agents, to uncover issues not raised by the agents, and to discover if contradictions exist between consumer and agent perspectives.

Participants in the focus groups tended to emphasize agent honesty and reliability as major themes in generating customer satisfaction. Integrity and trust were critical issues. In some cases, participants expressed a desire to accept what was perceived to be an honest, sensible, and cost-effective alternative without involving themselves in the technical details of the policies.

Satisfaction with a Health Care Center
Developing Preliminary Performance Attributes
Based on Customer Focus Groups

A health care center wished to determine performance attributes to measure satisfaction using a series of focus groups with former patients of the center. In this case, satisfaction of former patients, although critical, was only one facet in the total satisfaction process. Other aspects included satisfaction among doctors who influence recommendations and referrals, third-party payers, and family members of patients.

Differences among types of patients also influenced the determination of performance attributes. The requirements of emergency room patients and outpatients differ substantially from the requirements of patients with prolonged stays at a hospital.

The objective of these focus group discussions was to concentrate on satisfaction with the humanistic aspects under management control rather than on the technical quality of the health care center. Expectations about actual treatments or medical progress were omitted from the research.

Patients who had had health care stays of from two days to two weeks were invited to the focus groups. The focus groups generated the ideas presented in Exhibit 5.2. These ideas formed the basis for the development of a mail questionnaire that was sent to all patients who had been discharged after spending at least one night in the center.

Timing of the questionnaire mailing was very important. Patient recollection is greatest immediately after discharge, of course, but patients who are still very ill when returning home may disregard a mail questionnaire. These facts had to be considered in deciding on a time to mail questionnaires to the discharged patients.

Exhibit 5.2

Preliminary Performance Attributes: A Health Care Center

Overall Impression
Caring climate
Perception of value
Cleanliness
Technology

Admitting Procedures
Simplicity of procedures
Courteous treatment by admitting personnel
Reasonable length of time for admittance
Responses to all questions

Technical Services
Reasonable waiting time
Courteous personnel
Consideration for patients' comfort
Advance explanation of procedures

Food
Quality
Timeliness
Selection
Availability of special diets

Room
Ready upon arrival
Furniture functional for the purpose
Room kept clean
Room temperature appropriate
Room not noisy

Nursing Staff
Sensitive to patients' needs
Caring
Competent
Responsive to requests for help

Discharge Procedures
Procedures explained
Courteous employees
No unexpected delays

Billing
Correct
Responsive

Medical Staff
Explained scheduled tests and treatments

C A S E   S T U D Y

Satisfaction with a Package Delivery Company
Developing Preliminary Performance Attributes
Based on Customers' Assessment of Importance

The performance attributes in Exhibit 5.3 are at a much later stage of development than those in Exhibits 5.1 and 5.2. Executive interviews and customer focus groups have already been conducted. The ideas and concepts gleaned from them have been recorded as formal performance attributes using the words and perceptions expressed by the customers.

The potential attributes have been divided into six major categories: capability attributes, humanistic attributes, mechanistic attributes, interactive attributes, employee attributes, and competitive attributes. Nineteen major subcategories include geographic coverage, transit times, equipment and facilities, and the like.

The most important concepts were included in the final version of the customer satisfaction survey. Importance was determined by conducting a telephone survey of 300 customers. The list in Exhibit 5.3 was randomized so similar attributes did not necessarily follow each other during the interview. The statistical techniques of factor analysis and discriminant analysis (discussed in Chapter 11) were used in making the final selection of performance attributes.

This research project is an example of a rather lengthy process for determining critical performance. The customer satisfaction research

Exhibit 5.3

Preliminary Performance Attributes:
A Package Delivery Company

CAPABILITY FACTORS

Geographic Coverage
Geographic coverage is the most complete.
Geographic coverage meets business requirements.
Geographic coverage is better than competitors.

Transit Times
Shipping time is faster than competitors.
Agreed-upon shipping times are met.
Promised shipping times are guaranteed.

Equipment and Facilities
Equipment is modern and up-to-date.
Physical facilities are visually appealing.
Equipment satisfies customer requirements.

HUMANISTIC FACTORS

Responsiveness
Workers respond to questions quickly.
Workers respond to questions in a timely manner.

Dependability/Reliability
Personnel are very reliable.
Personnel keep their word when they make promises.
Personnel always provide services when promised.

Problem Handling
Problems are handled effectively as they arise.
Employees are understanding when problems arise.

MECHANISTIC FACTORS

Pickup
Pickup is prompt.
Pickup occurs when promised.
Customers are informed when pickup will occur.

Delivery

Delivery is prompt.
Delivery occurs when promised.
Customers are informed when delivery will occur.

Billing

Billing procedures are simple.
Billing procedures are accurate.

Tracking

Shipment tracking is easy.
Shipment tracking is timely.
Shipment tracking is accurate.
Shipment tracking exceeds competitors' capabilities.

Incidence of Damage

Damaged shipment occurrences are fewer than competitors'.
Level of damaged shipment occurrences is acceptable.

Damage-Claim Handling

Claims are handled promptly.
Claims are handled fairly.

INTERACTIVE FACTORS

Carrier/Shipper Interaction

Carrier acts like it wants the customer's business.
Carrier is willing to learn individual needs of the shipper.
Carrier is willing to adjust company procedures to meet individual needs of the customer.
Carrier helps shipper keep its costs down.

Communications

Services and policies are communicated to the customer.
Customers are well informed about matters concerning them.

EMPLOYEE FACTORS

Employees

Employees are neat and appropriately dressed.

continued

Employees are willing to go out of their way to help a customer.

Employees are trustworthy.

Employees are polite.

Upper management provides excellent support to employees.

Employees respect the customer.

Employees are willing to provide individual attention to the customer.

Employees know the needs of the customer.

Sales Representatives

Sales representatives are very helpful.

Sales representatives seem to care about customers' business.

Sales representatives are accessible when customers need them.

Sales representatives are responsive.

Sales representatives really understand shipping.

Sales representatives keep in touch with customers.

Sales representatives have the necessary technical skills.

Office Personnel

Office personnel are responsive.

Office personnel are helpful.

Office personnel are courteous.

Office personnel care about customers' business.

Drivers

Drivers are courteous.

Drivers are helpful.

Drivers are responsive.

COMPETITIVE FACTORS

Rates/Discounts

Volume discounts are negotiated fairly.

System for establishing rates is easy to understand.

Shipping rates are the lowest.

Shipping rates are competitive.

was viewed as the basis for developing a total quality management process. The performance attributes were used not only to determine customer satisfaction, but also to aid in the development of advanced mathematical models of customer behavior. Total quality management is discussed in Chapter 13, and modeling techniques are discussed in Chapter 11.

Image Attributes and Transaction Attributes

The performance attributes listed in Exhibits 5.1 and 5.3 were developed to capture information about a continuing relationship between the company and its customers. The utility company in Exhibit 5.1, for example, includes themes about overall service, social responsibility, and community involvement.

These "image"-related performance attributes are in contrast to "transaction"-based attributes that relate to only one instance in a relationship between the company and the customer. Here are a few examples of customers' recollections of individual transactions:

> I called the billing department with a question and she said 'If you don't want to pay the bill, we will see you in court' and hung up.

> The delay in admitting was terrible. I was in pain and they had some kind of computer problem. They came up with something saying I had just been born. They thought it was funny but I was in pain. I would not go back there again.

> The sales rep told us we were just a small account and were not important to him like, say, Westinghouse was. Since then he has been promoted to district sales manager. It's scary.

Every contact with the customer is referred to as a *transaction*. Transaction attributes are concerned with how a single contact is perceived. The little cards inquiring about satisfaction with a meal at a restaurant or a visit to a hotel are usually oriented toward transaction-based attributes. The attributes that will be developed based on the information in Exhibit 5.2 will tend to be transaction-based, since the health care center is focusing on the patient's recent visit.

Transaction-based surveys are usually narrower in focus than image-based surveys. The service department of an automobile dealership, for example, might conduct a satisfaction survey after a specific service transaction. The questions would refer to that particular instance of service:

Was the service completed on time?

Was the amount of the bill within the estimated amount?

Did the performed service actually resolve the problem?

Was the customer treated in a courteous manner?

Was the explanation of what was needed to be done understandable?

Many of the questions in a transaction-based survey are to be answered by either "yes" or "no." Negative responses can be followed by an open-ended question requesting more details about an unfavorable transaction. An image-based study, in contrast, inquires about opinions based on numerous transactions.

Most organizations require both image-related and transaction-related feedback about customer satisfaction. Overall satisfaction is most likely based on satisfaction with a series of individual transactions. Identifying and correcting transaction-related problems tends to improve the image-related view of satisfaction. A utility company, for example, may want information about a customer's satisfaction with a specific instance of service. A package delivery company might collect opinions about how an individual shipment was handled.

A customer's image-related satisfaction may be based on the experience of a single transaction. The transaction might not even be indicative of the current policies and practices of the organization. For example, here are three comments taken from recent customer satisfaction studies:

My daughter had an allergy and she was treated there 37 years ago and the treatment was bad. They hollered and yelled at my daughter, who was deathly afraid of a needle and, because of what they did, I would never go there again. I'm sure the people have changed but I still would never go there.

I won't go there because, back many years ago, in the Depression, they were the only bank that foreclosed on houses in our neighborhood.

I wouldn't want one. I had one and it didn't work very well. Of course, that was 23 years ago, but I don't think they are any better. Nothing else is.

Although these are extreme examples, similar themes occur with surprising regularity in customer satisfaction surveys. An important aspect of transaction-based surveys is the determination of the consequences of a good or bad transaction relative to overall satisfaction. Will one or two poor transactions, for example, permanently damage a long-term image? Conversely, will a few good transactions translate into a more loyal customer?

Customers' perceptions change as experiences with a company or product are accumulated. A long-distance telephone carrier, for example, might conduct an initial transaction-based survey to determine if equipment installation was completed as promised. A later image survey would inquire about clarity of connections, billing accuracy, handling of service problems, and other aspects of a long-term relationship. As another example, a consumer's views about a new automobile may change as experience with the vehicle is accumulated over time.

Combining image- and transaction-related performance attributes in a single survey must be done with extreme care. Survey participants find such shifts in emphasis confusing and difficult to respond to. It has been found that a few transaction-based questions can be successfully added to the end of an image-based survey. Similarly, a transaction-based survey can begin or end with a few general image questions. The distinction between the two types of questions, however, must be clear to the respondent.

Differences in Value-Added and Commodity Markets

Understanding the nature of the specific market in question is vital to customer satisfaction research. Critical performance attributes, for example, will differ in value-added and commodity markets. In a *value-added market*, customers pay a premium for experience, expertise, reputation, and superior quality. In this market outstanding service and rapid problem resolution should be important performance attributes. Customers in a generic *commodity market*, on the other hand, view products and services as interchangeable among suppliers. Price is a major concern in such a market.

Listening to customers' definitions of requirements may provide surprising results. One company, convinced that price was secondary to outstanding service, took for granted the value-added nature of its product. As its market share declined, the firm initiated a customer satisfaction study. Here are a few actual customer responses from the study that illustrate a recurring theme about the declining sales:

> A competitor offered a better price. We go by price.

> We switched because a competitor gave us the best price. Hey, if _____ would give us the same price, I would go back to them. That's it.

> They only give us a 35 percent volume discount. A competitor gives 53 percent. It's a question of dollars and cents.

> The price is better somewhere else. That's pretty much the bottom line.

A service company, on the other hand, consistently scored excellent satisfaction ratings although its price was definitely not the lowest. The perception of the company as a value-added supplier was obvious from comments explaining the high ratings:

> I have asked them to do nearly the impossible and they have been able to pull it off.

We get results, not excuses.

Whenever there is a problem, they respond. The customer comes first.

On Sunday they did a delivery for me when they were closed—that impressed me.

The manager is the friendliest and most wonderful man in the world. He works above and beyond the call of duty.

It is clear, then, that customers' perceptions help to define the success of a product or service, and that manufacturing and marketing strategies must consider customers' viewpoints.

Research Differences between Determining Performance Attributes and Measuring Satisfaction

A large portion of this book is devoted to explaining methodologies for developing questionnaires and analyzing survey results. The material can be used both to determine the critical performance attributes and to measure customer satisfaction. Important differences, however, exist between these two phases of customer satisfaction research.

Techniques used to analyze research data differ between the performance attribute definition phase and the satisfaction measurement phase. Special concerns associated with defining performance attributes are discussed in this chapter, and the analysis of satisfaction data is elaborated on in Chapters 9, 10, and 11.

Performance attribute definition must focus on expressing requirements and expectations in the customer's own vocabulary. Open-ended questions are especially suitable in this phase because they capture the instinctive diction and the spontaneity of the customer. These questions also eliminate a problem inherent with closed-ended questions: The set of alternatives may be inappropriate or incomplete.

Research indicates that customers will respond to inappropriate or incomplete preselected closed-ended responses if those are the only alternatives provided. Experiments have further shown that the preselected alternatives account for only about half of the pertinent information that could be generated if open-ended questions were used. Because capturing all of the relevant information is critical in defining appropriate performance attributes, open-ended questions are recommended in this phase.

Closed-ended questions, on the other hand, are appropriate for measuring and monitoring satisfaction after the performance attributes have been defined. The closed-ended format is ideal for quantifying results and measuring changes over time.

Schuman and Presser present a detailed discussion of the merits and drawbacks of open- and closed-ended questions. Geer (1988) offers a good discussion of open-ended questions. Critics of open-ended questions sometimes suggest that responses are superficial and fail to capture the salient issues from the customer's perspective. Geer (1991) concludes that open-ended responses do reflect these crucial issues.

Action Plan for Determining Critical Performance Attributes

An action plan for determining the critical performance attributes for a product or service is composed of five essential steps:

1. Communicate the intent of the research.
   a. Publicize and discuss with employees the reasons for the customer satisfaction research. Do not allow rumors to begin because employees were not told why questions are being asked.
   b. Discuss the motivation for the research with major customers and solicit their cooperation.

2. Perform internal research.
   a. Talk with the firm's executives, sales representatives, and customer service personnel.
   b. Study letters of praise and letters of complaint.
   c. Become familiar with the trends in indirect measures of customer satisfaction.
   d. Solicit information from all levels of the organization.

e. Plan how the various levels of the organization will obtain and use the survey results.

f. Use participation to obtain a commitment to the project methodology and results.

3. Perform qualitative research with customers.
   a. Define the firm's customers.
   b. Develop discussion guides for focus groups or in-depth interviews with customers.
   c. Conduct the research.
   d. Develop preliminary performance attributes using the vocabulary, wording, and terminology used by the customers.

4. Perform quantitative research with customers.
   a. Formulate objectives using information from the qualitative research.
   b. Develop the survey instrument.
   c. Conduct the research.
   d. Develop the critical performance attributes from the set of preliminary attributes established in Step 3.

5. Review results with the organization.
   a. Review the results with customers and employees.
   b. Modify and enhance the performance attributes.
   c. Finalize the list of performance attributes.

6

Mail or Telephone Survey?

*T*elephone interviews and mail questionnaires are the chief methods of collecting data for customer satisfaction research. A choice must be made between these two methods before the research process can proceed.

Each of these two methods has its advantages and its disadvantages, all of which must be evaluated in order to determine which method will be used. It is possible, also, that using both types of surveys may be the best decision.

Factors in Selecting the Appropriate Survey Method

The criteria for a specific research project—time restrictions, cost, confidentiality, and the like—will determine whether a telephone survey or a mail questionnaire is the more appropriate means of collecting data in customer satisfaction research.

Telephone surveys are usually more desirable because they permit superior quality control, a reduction in nonresponse bias (discussed in the following section), a faster turnaround time, and an opportunity to direct open-ended responses.

Mail surveys are justified if the customers are difficult to reach by telephone or if the budget cannot support telephone interviewing. Mail surveys can also be effective if a very long list of attributes is involved (for example, in examining the importance of various performance attributes).

Certain research data are difficult to obtain with telephone interviews. Conjoint analysis (see Chapter 11) and psychographic (lifestyle) data, for example, are usually obtained using mail or in-person surveys. This type of information, however, is usually not collected in customer satisfaction research. Mail surveys may become more desirable as conjoint analysis and psychographic data become integrated with customer satisfaction research.

A limited budget is the least justifiable reason for conducting a mail survey. Inaccurate or misleading information is not desirable at any savings in cost. The extra effort required to reduce nonresponse bias will also significantly increase the cost of a mail survey.

An excellent introduction to mail surveys is presented by Erdos, to telephone surveys by Frey, and to both mail and telephone surveys by Dillman.

Response Rates and Nonresponse Bias

Mail Surveys

Typical response rates for mail questionnaires are in the 20 percent to 30 percent range unless specific actions are taken to increase the number of returns. These low response rates can significantly distort the survey results.

In data collection research, bias occurs when data show a persistent tendency away from the true value of the population parameter. A nonresponse bias is introduced in mail surveys because customers who are interested in the survey are more likely to respond than customers who are not. The opinions of customers who take the time and effort to return the questionnaire are often quite different from the opinions of customers who ignore the survey. For example, response rates for consumer-oriented mail surveys tend to be higher among better-educated and higher-income customers.

Proponents of mail surveys often claim that statistically valid results are possible because the number of completed interviews is large. Unless the response rate is exceptionally high, however, nonresponse bias is always a potential problem.

To illustrate, 900 returned surveys from a mailing to 9,000 customers (10 percent response) is not equivalent to 900 questionnaires obtained from a telephone survey of 1,000 customers (90 percent response). Nonresponse bias is reinforced, not reduced, if additional surveys are obtained using the same procedures that created the bias.

Consistency of results over several quarters is also no guarantee that validity has been achieved. Biased results are likely to be repeated if the source of the bias is repeated. Reliability does not infer validity.

The effects of nonresponse in mail surveys can be minimized by using two strategies: (1) use procedures known to increase response rates and (2) estimate the amount and direction of the bias created by the nonresponses.

In the first strategy, the cover letter is critical to the success of any mail survey. The cover letter, written on the sponsoring company's letterhead, must clearly indicate the purpose of the survey, how the recipient was chosen, and why participation is important and beneficial. The following example contains the essential elements of an effective cover letter.

Dear [Customer]:

Your satisfaction is very important to _____.
We are dedicated to continuing to improve our products and services and to better satisfy your requirements. Please take three minutes to give us some feedback on how we are doing now and how we can improve in the future.

The enclosed survey was mailed to a scientifically selected random sample of our customers. Your participation is very important because your reply will represent about two hundred other businesses like yours. We will use the results to develop strategies and plans to offer you better products and services.

Your responses are completely confidential. That is why the enclosed reply envelope is addressed to _____.
They will process the questionnaires and give us the results but will omit the customers' names. Please be frank and open in answering the questions.

Please take a few minutes to complete the questionnaire right now, if you can. If you can't, I would appreciate your response before July 15.

If you have any questions or concerns, call us toll free at 1-800-XXX-XXXX. Thank you for your help.

Sincerely,

President

Several standard procedures can increase response rates for mail questionnaires. The following techniques may be helpful, depending on the type of satisfaction study being conducted:

1. Obtain the name of the appropriate person to complete the mail questionnaire. A personalized letter will increase the response rate.

2. Follow-up letters or telephone calls, requesting completion of the survey, can be sent routinely to all recipients of the questionnaire. Here is a typical example of a follow-up request:

    You received a very important questionnaire from us about one week ago. If you have already returned the questionnaire, we thank you very much. If not, please take a few minutes now to complete the survey. Your opinions are very important to us. If you need another copy of the questionnaire, please call us toll-free at 1-800-XXX-XXXX.

Twenty percent is a typical response rate for the first follow-up. An additional 10 percent can be expected for a second follow-up.

3. Returns can be coded so that second and third requests can be directed only to customers that have not responded. Requests can be either by mail or telephone.

4. Customers can be supplied with a postcard that they can mail separate from the survey, indicating that the questionnaire has been returned. This reinforces the confidentiality of the survey.

5. Customers can be offered an incentive for completing the survey. Research has shown that enclosing a cash payment (for example, a dollar bill) tends to increase the response rate. Although effective with consumers, this technique may be counterproductive in business-to-business studies. Executives, for example, might feel insulted if the implication is that their time is only worth one dollar. The cover letter should always emphasize that the payment is a token of appreciation rather than a payment for services.

   Cash is not the only incentive that can be offered. Physicians have responded to surveys that included inexpensive devices that can be useful in their work. A donation to charity is another alternative. Numerous research studies have shown, however, that an enclosed gift increases response rates much more than a promise to provide a payment or gift (even if the promised gift is much greater in value than the enclosed gift).

   Offering to send respondents a summary of the survey results is also an effective incentive. This option, however, is not recommended with customer satisfaction studies because of the proprietary nature of the research.

6. Return envelopes with postage stamps usually get better responses than envelopes with a postage paid permit. Hensley found that the type of stamp (metered, "regular," or "commemorative" first-class) influenced the response rate. Furthermore, using different types of stamps on the outer envelope and on the return mail envelope increased the response rate even more.

Customer interest in the subject matter is probably the most important factor in determining response rates. Questionnaires mailed to individuals with little interest in the subject tend to be disregarded and not returned.

It is informative to conduct a statistical analysis comparing the number of initial responses with the number of responses obtained after actions were initiated to increase the response rate. Although not precise, the statistical analysis can provide insight into the bias associated with nonresponse.

Research by Goodstadt, Chung, Kronitz, and Cook found that early returns tended to exhibit more favorable opinions than later returns did. This suggests that the opinions of nonrespondents could be even less favorable. A somewhat surprising additional result of the study was that *very* late returns also demonstrated favorable opinions.

Telephone Surveys

Telephone survey response rates can exceed 90 percent for business-to-business satisfaction surveys and 85 percent for consumer surveys. This is especially true if the name of the sponsoring company is identified.

One company obtained a 27 percent response rate for a mail questionnaire concerning employee satisfaction with a training program. A telephone survey concerning the same subject resulted in 400 completed interviews with only one refusal.

Refusals, of course, are only one form of nonresponse. Other contributors to nonresponse bias in telephone surveys are failure to reach the customer, unlisted telephone numbers, and answering machines. Each of these contributors is discussed in this section.

Refusals. Refusals may not create nonresponse bias if the reason for the refusal is unrelated to the content of the survey. A subtle bias, however, may still exist. For example, when a satisfaction study is conducted in both urban and rural areas, refusal rates are much higher in the urban areas. The results can therefore easily be biased toward rural areas if attention is not given to the geographic areas in which the refusals are occurring.

Research by DeMaio of the Census Bureau indicated that

West Coast states produced the highest refusal rates, and Southern states had the highest cooperation rate. Although the Census Bureau research was concerned with the general public, the same pattern has been observed in business-to-business studies.

Although the Census Bureau reported no differences in refusal rates by either race or sex, and income was not included in the analysis, other studies have concluded that refusal rates are greater among whites and higher-income residents. Additional information about response rates is found in Sudman and in Wiseman and McDonald.

No Answer. Failure to reach a customer is another form of nonresponse bias associated with telephone surveys. About one-third to one-half of the general public is typically not at home at any one time. Callback procedures must be implemented to reach more customers. Otherwise, the results will be biased toward easier-to-reach customers such as retired or unemployed individuals, mothers with small children, and households with a large number of people.

Unlisted Telephone Numbers. Samples drawn from telephone directories are becoming less reliable due to increases in unlisted telephone numbers. Over one-half of the households in some metropolitan areas now have unlisted telephone numbers. Las Vegas leads the nation with a 57 percent unlisted rate. Unlisted numbers in California are quite common. In fact, of the 15 metropolitan areas with the highest percentage of unlisted numbers, 11 are in California. Low-income minorities are the demographic group with the highest percentage of unlisted telephone numbers.

Survey research companies often use a technique called random-digit dialing to compensate for the problems encountered with telephone directories. Although the technical details are complex, the basic idea is to generate four random numbers and append them to an area code and exchange. The random generation will include numbers that do not appear in telephone directories.

The technique of random-digit dialing will, unfortunately, also include business and disconnected telephone numbers along with numbers that may never have existed. However, companies specializing in the development of random-digit numbers have methods of screening out many of these unwanted numbers.

Use of random-digit dialing will also increase the representation of new listings that have not been published in directories. Because approximately 20 percent of the population changes residences in a year, telephone directories are outdated rapidly. Relying on directories will produce samples that significantly underestimate the importance of renters, since renters tend to move more often than home owners.

In general, random-digit dialing is very important in marketing research. However, because names of customers are usually known in satisfaction surveys, the technique is often of lesser importance in such research. Random-digit dialing is discussed in detail in Lavrakas and in Frey.

Answering Machines. Reducing the nonresponse bias created by answering machines requires both planning and persistence. About 25 percent of the population owns an answering machine, and use of the machine is more prevalent on the weekends. A recent study by Tuckel and Feinberg concluded that most respondents with answering machines were reachable if enough callbacks were conducted. Callbacks must be attempted at different times and on different days. The answering machines apparently were not used to screen 100 percent of the calls. Once respondents with answering machines were reached, the individuals were generally willing to participate in the survey.

Statistically weighting survey results to adjust for nonresponse is recommended by some researchers. Fuller and Mandell both provide good introductions to the subject of weighting survey results.

Which Is Best?

There are a number of procedures and methodologies that may result in the collection of similar research information. Each procedure or methodology has its own advantages and disadvantages.

A mail survey might be used if a large number of customers are inaccessible by telephone, if cost is a consideration, and if lifestyle data are particularly important. A telephone survey might be chosen to reduce nonresponse bias or to obtain fast responses. A telephone survey is the best choice if the supervision of open-ended responses is critical.

7

Designing the Questionnaire

Questionnaire design is a critical phase of the customer satisfaction research process. It has been said that a survey is only as good as the questions it asks.

Preparing an effective questionnaire requires both experience and patience. Many businesspeople consider the construction of a questionnaire to be a relatively simple, straightforward task. The truth is that it is exceptionally difficult to create a questionnaire that is both accurate and relevant. The skillful preparation of such a questionnaire will contribute significantly to the success of the research.

Certain structural aspects of questionnaires are generic and standardized. Some sections, however, must be customized in order to capture the distinctive characteristics of the organization and its industry. Decisions must be made about the use of

71

open- and closed-ended questions. Open-ended questions may generate more information than closed-ended questions, but they also require more time to develop, administer, and analyze.

The wording of questions is critical, and proper questionnaire wording is considered an art. An improperly worded questionnaire will not achieve the desired results and can lead to incorrect interpretations. Guidelines and principles of questionnaire wording will be presented in this chapter.

A Generic Customer Satisfaction Survey

An outline of a generic customer satisfaction telephone survey is presented in Exhibit 7.1. The survey contains two major components:

1. Overall satisfaction ratings for ten companies—the sponsoring company and nine major competitors
2. Performance ratings on individual attributes for the sponsoring company and two major competitors

Information should be obtained for two or three major competitors. Performance ratings are easier to interpret if they are compared with scores of the competition. Improvement over time should also be compared against changes in the competitors' scores.

Management of the sponsoring company usually selects the competitors to appear in the survey. An alternative is to ask the customer what competing products or services he or she uses. For example:

What dishwashing soaps have you used in the last three months?

The interviewer can then inquire about the sponsoring company and the first two or three competitors. This alternative provides good results in situations where the competition is not defined precisely or where the competition varies significantly in different geographic locations. The survey, however, may be dif-

Exhibit 7.1

Customer Satisfaction Questionnaire: Generic Outline

Using a scale from 1 to 5, where 5 means very satisfied and 1 means not satisfied at all, how do you rate the following companies?

____ Company A	____ Company F
____ Company B	____ Company G
____ Company C	____ Company H
____ Company D	____ Company I
____ Company E	____ Company J

Using the same 5-point scale, how do you rate:

	Company A	Company B	Company C
Performance attribute 1	____	____	____
Performance attribute 2	____	____	____
Performance attribute 3	____	____	____
Performance attribute 4	____	____	____
Performance attribute 5	____	____	____
Performance attribute 6	____	____	____
Performance attribute 7	____	____	____
Performance attribute 8	____	____	____
Performance attribute 9	____	____	____
Performance attribute 10	____	____	____

ficult to administer and the results may also be difficult to tabulate and analyze.

Questions about overall satisfaction are asked before questions about individual performance attributes. This follows the accepted rule that general questions should precede specific questions.

Respondents may give less thoughtful answers to questions near the end of a long list. This potential bias is reduced by asking the questions in a random order. The generic customer satisfaction survey contains two lists that should be randomized: the companies in the overall satisfaction section and the individual performance attributes in the second section.

Randomization is easily accomplished when computer-assisted interviewing technology is used. Note that randomization is not possible with a mail questionnaire unless different versions of the survey are distributed.

The survey in Exhibit 7.1 can be completed in about four minutes. Several significant enhancements can be made to this basic survey. Each enhancement, however, will increase cost and consume more of the respondent's time.

Enhancements to the Generic Questionnaire

Satisfaction may not be a completely reliable predictor of future purchasing decisions. Two additional indicators, measuring product or service loyalty, are often included in customer satisfaction surveys:

1. The likelihood of repurchasing the product or service
2. The likelihood of recommending the product or service to friends or business associates

Three additional enhancements are discussed in the following sections of this chapter: Open-ended questions, the inclusion of questions concerning individual customer expectations, and the development of procedures to rectify specific customer problems.

Questions relating to demographics should be included in the survey. Business-to-business studies, for example, might capture information about the customer's total sales, type of industry, and geographic region. Satisfaction could differ substantially between small and large customers or between customers in the chemical and automotive markets. In fact, the performance attributes that create satisfaction may be different among these groups.

Demographics for consumer studies usually include information about age, household income, sex, and education. This information may be important in the initial development of performance attributes as well as in the analysis of the survey results. For example, purchasers of automobiles in different geographic regions will have different requirements about resistance to salt and winter weather.

Marketing research is often concerned with psychographic as well as demographic information. Psychographics involve the study of customer values, attitudes, and lifestyle characteristics as they relate to purchase behavior. Demographics deal with facts, whereas psychographics are concerned with attitudes and feelings.

Questionnaires developed to collect psychographic information often contain a series of lifestyle statements. Respondents use a scale ranging from "strongly agree" to "strongly disagree" to describe their view of each statement. A toy manufacturer, for example, may hypothesize that adult satisfaction with a child's toy is related to the toy's educational value. Such psychographic questions are included in a satisfaction survey to capture the parent's aspirations for the child. The survey is attempting to discover not only the level of satisfaction with the product but the reason why the satisfaction has occurred.

Psychographic information is usually not incorporated in satisfaction surveys, since psychographic questions are not considered compatible with satisfaction questions. This view may change as the sophistication of customer satisfaction research increases.

Open-Ended Questions

Open-ended questions are questions that ask the respondent to answer in his or her own words. *Closed-ended questions,* by contrast, are questions that ask the respondent to choose from specific, predefined answers, giving the one that is closest to his or her own viewpoint.

Both open- and closed-ended questions are important in customer satisfaction research. The balance between the two types of questions is an important aspect of questionnaire design.

Open-ended questions enhance a survey's usefulness and value. The responses to these questions clarify the reasons for "very poor" or "very good" ratings. A utility company, for example, might follow up a very poor rating with the following:

You gave the power company a very poor rating with regard to concern for environmental impact. Please tell us why you feel that way.

Open-ended responses provide a warning signal that certain questions have been misunderstood by the respondent. For example, a question intending to determine how a mortgage broker was identified and selected was answered as follows:

Interviewer: How did you find the mortgage broker?
Respondent: Very helpful.

Even if the intent of the question is clear, respondents sometimes reverse the rating scale, indicating "very satisfied" with a "1" instead of a "5." Responses to open-ended questions provide a clue before the survey is completed that a misunderstanding has occurred.

If the survey involves a large number of interviews, a sample of questions can be selected for open-ended elaborations. For example, suppose that a questionnaire contains 10 open-ended questions and the survey involves 2,000 interviews. If each customer is asked 2 open-ended questions, then a total of 400 responses would be generated for each of the 10 questions. This strategy is especially effective if computer-assisted interviewing is used, since the computer can select the questions in a randomized manner.

Computer-assisted interviewing can also be used to select open-ended questions based on responses to a sequence of questions. For example, additional competitive intelligence can be gained by implementing the following procedures:

- If a major competitor scores higher on overall satisfaction or on a critical performance attribute, an open-ended question can be asked to clarify why that company is viewed more favorably.

- If three major competitors all receive identical scores on overall satisfaction, the customer can be asked to compare the strengths and weaknesses of the three companies.

A survey should close with an open-ended question to capture any thoughts that were not captured during the survey. For example: "What else would you like to add that has not been covered in our survey?" The question should not be phrased "Is there anything else?" because the customer will most likely say "no."

Guidelines for Asking Open-Ended Questions

Three guidelines concerning open-ended question research should be followed in the development and implementation of effective questions:

1. Alternatives should not be suggested in the question or by the interviewer. Bias will be introduced if the customer is led or prompted into a response, as in this example:

   Interviewer: How would you rate _____
   on "helps make the community a better place to live"?
   Customer: I'm not sure what you mean by that.
   Interviewer: Well, you know, like sponsoring ballets and things like that.

   Interviewers should not offer explanations unless the explanations are given to every respondent. If a respondent has difficulty interpreting a question, the interviewer should ask the respondent to give the best interpretation he or she can and should not supply additional information.

   The troublesome question should be changed if a significant number of customers have difficulty with interpretation. This problem is usually identified if the survey is adequately pretested.

2. Responses must be recorded verbatim. Comments should not be edited or summarized by the interviewer. Bias will be introduced if the quality of each interviewer's editing skills is introduced into a response.

   Here is an example taken from a training session in which an experienced project manager was monitoring a telephone interviewer to compare actual customer responses with the responses recorded by the interviewer:

Customer: It goes back to the claim we had because there were a number of problems. I mean, it took about two, well over two weeks to even arrange an inspection of the merchandise. No one at the office was able to help us. I mean, you would call up and they would say someone will call you back and they never would call back. They just didn't make a lot of effort to help us in that manner.

Interviewer: It goes back to a claim we had, took over two weeks, no one at the office seemed to put a lot of effort into it.

The fact that the arrangement for inspection was what took over two weeks was completely lost in the translation. Also, the failure to return telephone calls is not included in the interviewer's version of the conversation.

Accuracy and reliability are suspect if open-ended responses are not recorded as verbatim responses. For example, "She said that the guarantee was the most important aspect of her buying decision" is not a verbatim response.

3. The interviewer must have the skill and experience to probe a response for additional detail and clarification. Consider how much additional information was gained with the following four examples of probing:

a. CUSTOMER: The service isn't that good.

   INTERVIEWER: Could you give me an example of why the service isn't that good?

   CUSTOMER: They are not open after 6 o'clock on Friday evening and that's when I do my banking.

b. CUSTOMER: I gave them a high rating because of the cooperation I receive.

   INTERVIEWER: Could you give me an example of the cooperation you receive?

   CUSTOMER: They help explain the bills and always deliver on time.

c. CUSTOMER: They gave us the best deal.

INTERVIEWER: What do you mean by "the best deal"?

CUSTOMER: We got a 35 percent discount and the best I could get from competitors was 28 percent.

d. CUSTOMER: We're a new business and we just got started.

INTERVIEWER: What made you decide to use our company?

CUSTOMER: I had heard good things about your company.

INTERVIEWER: What good things have you heard?

CUSTOMER: I heard you are easy to deal with.

INTERVIEWER: What else did you hear?

CUSTOMER: I heard that the service is very professional.

INTERVIEWER: How is the service professional?

CUSTOMER: If I need to call the office with a question or problem, I hear I get an answer right away—not all this running-around business.

Appropriate probing is very important to understanding the expectations, requirements, and experiences of the customer. An interviewer shouldn't settle for open-ended responses like:

The other companies are doing a better job.

I don't care for them.

Because of the military.

I prefer to use other companies.

Because of the manager.

They don't do what they say.

They were good but I am not happy with them now.

We had a problem with a sales rep.

They do a good job.

Open-ended questions and prompts that begin with the word *why* can be counterproductive because defensive barriers are often created when the word is used. *Why* implies that a rational explanation should be provided. Opinions and attitudes are not always formed in a completely rational manner.

Closed-ended questions may also require a probe to clarify or categorize a response. For example:

a. CUSTOMER: I'll give them about a four and a half on that one.

INTERVIEWER: I'm sorry, I can't put in fractions. Is that closer to a 4 or to a 5?

b. INTERVIEWER: Would you say the technical support is very good, good, fair, or poor?

CUSTOMER: I would say not very good.

INTERVIEWER: Well, of the four categories I mentioned, which would best describe the technical support? Would you say very good, good, fair, or poor?

The interviewing process always introduces some amount of variability. Random variability tends to balance out. Because the effects of systematic bias introduced by differences in interviewing techniques will not balance, introductions, clarifications, and probing techniques must be standardized and continually monitored.

Some Examples. Everyone has seen a customer satisfaction questionnaire. Many restaurants, for example, solicit opinions about food and service with a little card accompanying the bill. Similar questionnaires are used by hotels, hospitals, car rental agencies, and numerous other businesses.

Hypothetical examples are shown in Exhibits 7.2 and 7.3. These questionnaires illustrate important points about the use of open- and closed-ended questions, the wording of a questionnaire, and measurement scales.

In Exhibit 7.2 the Red Dragon Restaurant uses open-ended questions to collect responses in the customers' own words. Responses in open-ended format can lead to insightful perspectives and can provide extremely beneficial information. The results, however, are difficult to quantify and monitor over time.

Responses to open-ended questions are sometimes viewed with skepticism because the ability to articulate a response will influence the quality of the answer. The response may be affected by the customer's level of education as well as by his or her opinions and attitudes.

In contrast, in Exhibit 7.3 the patrons of the River Resort Inn are asked to circle or check predefined responses:

Yes or no

Excellent, good, fair, or poor

Just right, too small, too large

These are closed-ended questions. The questions are easy to answer and tabulate, but they do not provide significant individual insights or informative details.

The examples in Exhibits 7.2 and 7.3 underscore the need to recognize, when preparing survey questions, that the ultimate value of customer satisfaction research lies in implementing action plans to improve performance. What action can the management of the two restaurants take based on the questionnaire results?

The River Resort Inn in Exhibit 7.3 should certainly improve service if "quality of service" consistently receives a poor rating. But how should service be improved? What service components need attention? If the menu selection is poor, how should it be changed? The answers will not be found by analyzing closed-ended responses for subjects as broad as service or menu selection.

The Red Dragon Restaurant in Exhibit 7.2 has a different set of problems. What standard will be used to quantify and track customer satisfaction over time? These difficulties are introduced by the complete reliance on open-ended questions.

Avoiding Bias. Care must be taken to avoid the introduction of bias in questionnaires. The opinions of the customers who take the time to fill out questionnaires such as those in Exhibits 7.2 and 7.3 will differ from those who do not. Research on this subject has shown that two groups tend to fill out self-administered questionnaires: very satisfied customers and very dissatisfied customers. Combining the opinions of these extreme groups does not average out to a representative middle point.

Bias can also be introduced if the questionnaire is poorly written or if telephone interviewers are inadequately trained or

---

Exhibit 7.2

Questionnaire Using Open-Ended Questions

THE RED DRAGON RESTAURANT

To assist us in better serving you, we would like you to answer the following questions:

1. How is our food quality? _____

2. How is our service attitude? _____

3. How is our cleanliness? _____

4. How are our prices? _____

5. New menu item suggestions: _____

6. How did you hear of us? _____

7. Other comments: _____

supervised. Other sources of bias are discussed throughout this book.

Individual Customer Expectations and Requirements

Computers can calculate average satisfaction ratings in a matter of seconds. Customers, however, do not think like computers. Overall satisfaction, from the customer's perspective, is not a weighted sum of the individual performance attribute ratings.

Unacceptable performance in a single facet of the customer / company relationship may result in a dissatisfied customer. The performance attribute that provokes the dissatisfaction may vary from customer to customer. For this reason, analyses that com-

---

Exhibit 7.3

Questionnaire Using Closed-Ended Questions

THE RIVER RESORT INN

Please take a few minutes to answer some questions that will help us improve our menu and service:

Were you greeted and made to feel welcome?   YES   NO
Were service personnel helpful and pleasant?   YES   NO

Quality of service was:
              EXCELLENT   GOOD   FAIR   POOR
Menu selection was:
              EXCELLENT   GOOD   FAIR   POOR
Quality of food/beverage was:
              EXCELLENT   GOOD   FAIR   POOR
How would you rate the atmosphere?
              EXCELLENT   GOOD   FAIR   POOR

Food/beverage portions were:
              JUST RIGHT   TOO SMALL   TOO LARGE
Prices of food/beverages were:
                          WHAT I EXPECTED
                          LOWER THAN EXPECTED
                          HIGHER THAN EXPECTED

Were prices reasonable for the value received?   YES   NO
Would you dine with us again?   YES   NO

COMMENTS: _____

_____

pare company performance to customer expectations and requirements on an individual basis can be very insightful.

These analyses are patterned after some of the earliest work in customer satisfaction research. Cardozo, for example, compared expectations prior to a purchase with the extent to which the expectations were satisfied after the purchase.

Two examples of questionnaire structure are presented in this section. Analysis techniques are discussed in Chapter 10.

Example 1: Importance and Satisfaction Ratings. Questions can be developed to obtain information about both the importance and the satisfaction associated with each performance attribute. The following structure, for example, was adopted by an insurance company:

Performance Attribute	Customer Importance	Customer Satisfaction
a. Ease of reaching a customer service representative	1 2 3 4 5	1 2 3 4 5
b. Courtesy of customer service representatives	1 2 3 4 5	1 2 3 4 5
c. 24-hour claim service	1 2 3 4 5	1 2 3 4 5
d. Timeliness of initial contact	1 2 3 4 5	1 2 3 4 5
e. Timeliness of claim payment	1 2 3 4 5	1 2 3 4 5
f. Billing accuracy	1 2 3 4 5	1 2 3 4 5
g. Quality of information booklets	1 2 3 4 5	1 2 3 4 5

Customer importance:
 1 = not at all important
 5 = extremely important

Customer satisfaction:
 1 = not at all satisfied
 5 = completely satisfied

Gaps between customer importance and customer satisfaction can be computed using this structure. Attributes where high importance is combined with poor performance carry top priority for corrective action.

The 1–5 rating scale can be unrealistic in some applications. Suppose that customers of an airline rated the importance of excellent meals, in-flight movies, variety of reading materials, and the competency of the pilot. A 1–5 measurement scale is not suitable for comparing requirements varying from reading materials to safety-of-life situations.

Another drawback to these analyses is that all of the performance attributes might be considered extremely important. This is especially true if the attributes were defined correctly in the initial stages of the research.

Example 2: Requirements and Satisfaction Ratings. The survey can be designed so that the customer defines the *requirements* for a performance attribute rather than the importance of the attribute. For example, the insurance satisfaction study could be modified as follows:

> In your opinion, what is an acceptable amount of time for completion of claim service?
>
> How satisfied are you that the company is providing claim service within that time? Are you very satisfied, somewhat satisfied, not very satisfied, or not at all satisfied?

This type of structure captures information about individual customer satisfaction. It also obtains additional information about performance requirements on an ongoing basis.

Another example is a variation of the two-question method to determine both individual requirements and satisfaction. Here a company provides sealants and adhesives to manufacturers of custom-made products. The manufacturers require fast responses to price quote inquiries, since this information must be included in calculating bids. The questionnaire structure for the requirement and satisfaction sequence is as follows:

A. To be responsive to your customers, how quickly do you need price quotes from our company?
   a. Immediately on the telephone
   b. Within one hour
   c. Within one to two hours
   d. Within three to four hours
   e. Within a day

B. How quickly does our company supply price quote information?
   a. Immediately on the telephone
   b. Within one hour
   c. Within one to two hours

d. Within three to four hours

e. Within a day

As customer satisfaction research matures, emphasis should shift from cross-sectional analyses at one point in time to comparisons of individual customer opinions over several time periods. The structures discussed here will accommodate such comparisons.

Feedback about Specific Customer Problems

Customers are usually guaranteed confidentiality when responding to a satisfaction survey. Not all customers, however, want to remain anonymous.

The survey methodology should provide opportunities to rectify specific problems or complications. The interviewer must ask permission to use the customer's name. For example:

CUSTOMER: I have never seen a sales rep but I am interested in talking with one. Maybe you can figure out a way of getting one out here.

INTERVIEWER: Would you like a representative of the _____ Company to follow this up with you?

CUSTOMER: I certainly would.

INTERVIEWER: May I use your name when I give the information to the _____ Company?

If this option is implemented, the mechanism to accurately record and follow up every request must be in place. Since expectations for follow-up and improvement have been created, failure to take action will only make the situation worse by creating a higher level of dissatisfaction.

The Survey Introduction

The survey introduction is very important to the ultimate success of the project. The introduction is contained in the cover letter for a mail survey. For a telephone survey, the first ten seconds of the interview often determine whether or not the customer will participate in the survey.

In a telephone survey, interviewers will require a general introduction to reach the right person. Depending on the information supplied, this introduction will be structured as follows:

> Hello, this is Ann from _____. May I speak with:
> —Mr. Thomas Smith.
> —the director of computer operations.
> —the person responsible for making decisions about computer equipment.

After reaching the appropriate person, the survey introduction should contain three major components:

1. Why the interview is being conducted

2. How the customer was selected

3. Why the customer should participate

For example:

> Hello, this is Ann from _____. We are talking with customers of _____ to get an idea of their satisfaction with _____. Your company was selected at random. Your opinions are very important to help _____ give you the best possible products and services.

The introduction must be delivered in a confident and professional manner. The length of the interview should not be mentioned unless the customer specifically asks for that information, and permission to conduct the interview should not be asked. Questions such as "Is this a convenient time?" are generally answered negatively, and the customer can be expected to inform the interviewer if the time is inconvenient.

The Wording of Questions

The effective wording of questions requires experience, skill, and attention to detail. It is, therefore, best accomplished by a professional marketing research organization.

In Exhibit 7.3, for example, the River Resort Inn question about quality of food and beverage combines two distinct thoughts in one question. How does a customer rate "quality of food/beverage" if the food was excellent but the beverage was poor? Does the food/beverage combination get a "fair" rating even though neither food nor beverage was considered fair? Should the combination get a "good" rating if the customer considered the food to be the more important part of the dinner?

Some customers will ignore the confusing question. Others might divide the food and beverage question into two parts and add additional information in the margin of the questionnaire. Such lack of uniformity in responses creates difficulties in analyzing and interpreting the survey results. Consequently, the owner of the River Resort Inn may form opinions based on inaccurate or misleading information.

In Exhibits 7.2 and 7.3, inquiries about price are handled very differently by the two restaurants. The Red Dragon's question ("How are our prices?") is actually very difficult to answer. What is the standard for comparison—another oriental restaurant, a fast-food restaurant, an expensive downtown restaurant? The River Resort Inn makes an attempt at addressing the comparison problem: "Were prices reasonable for the value received?"

Presented below are a few examples of ineffective questions and of performance attributes formulated by inexperienced questionnaire developers:

1. "Customer support personnel are courteous and knowledgeable."

   Two thoughts are combined in one attribute. How is the question to be answered if a respondent thinks the customer support personnel are very knowledgeable but not very courteous?

2. "Would you say that the customer support staff is always, almost always, sometimes, rarely, or never prompt in returning calls?"

When the performance attribute is mentioned last, the customer will have difficulty recalling the alternatives.

3. "The carrier must respond within five hours to calls for pickups."

Strongly Agree				Strongly Disagree
1	2	3	4	5

The wording and the measurement scale make a response difficult to interpret. Does a "strongly disagree" rating imply that the company must receive a response in less than five hours? How would the respondent answer this question if ten hours were considered adequate?

4. "Reason for calling customer service?"

Incomplete statements should be avoided. Someone is bound to change the wording of an incomplete statement so that a question can be answered. Either the interviewer or the respondent will provide his or her unique interpretation. To reduce this bias, standardization must be achieved. An improved version of this example is: "What was the reason for your last call to customer service?"

5. These two questions address the same performance attribute:
   a. "How satisfied are you with the availability of medical claim information?"
   b. "How satisfied are you that the company keeps you up to date on the status of a medical claim?"

Researchers have demonstrated that satisfaction ratings are significantly lower when questions are worded in an active manner, such as in the second option, than when the more passive tone of the first option is used.

These examples illustrate the care and expertise required to word questions properly. Payne's 1951 book, *The Art of Asking Questions,* is a classic in questionnaire wording. Converse and Presser's more recent text, *Survey Questions,* is devoted to the subject of wording questions.

Measurement Scales

Customer satisfaction or dissatisfaction is not directly observable in a telephone interview or a mail questionnaire. Customer perceptions must be quantified to measure satisfaction. The measurement process, therefore, is a critical component of the research. Quantification strategies based on poorly selected measurement scales may result in inaccurate and misleading conclusions.

Different measurement scales may appear in the same questionnaire. A yes–no scale, for example, is used if the question addresses an event that either occurred or did not occur.

- Were magazines distributed on the flight?
- Did you receive the shipment on time?
- Was the billing accurate?

Five-point scales are often used when responses involve attitudes or opinions rather than facts. For example:

a. Very satisfied	b. Excellent	c. Much better
Satisfied	Good	Better
Neutral	Average	About the same
Dissatisfied	Below average	Not as good
Very dissatisfied	Poor	Much worse

A three-point scale can be used if questions relate to specific performance requirements: exceeds requirements, meets requirements, does not meet requirements. Seven- and 10-point scales are also commonly used.

Some researchers use scales with an even number of alternatives (thereby eliminating the neutral middle point) to force respondents into a positive or negative view. Other researchers consider a neutral response as perfectly valid and object to measurement scales that eliminate this alternative.

There is a limit to the precision that respondents can furnish in answering questions that require a rating scale. Precision will not be increased if the number of alternatives exceeds the respondent's ability to distinguish or differentiate among the alternatives. Therefore a 7- or 10-point scale will not discriminate any better than a 5-point scale if respondents conceptualize answers on a 5-point scale. The average rating will vary more with an expanded scale, but the standard deviation will also increase.

The measurement scale used with closed-ended questions exemplifies another important factor in designing questionnaires. In Exhibit 7.3, the River Resort Inn considers "quality of service" to be an opinion. One of four responses is expected: excellent, good, fair, or poor. Whether or not a patron was greeted and made to feel welcome, however, is considered a fact that can be answered by either "yes" or "no." The quality of the greeting (excellent, good, fair, or poor) is not an issue.

The ratings of several performance attributes can be added together to form an index called a *summed rating scale*. Suppose, for example, that the human resources department of a company is responsible for humanistic issues involving interactions with customers (e.g., customer service), and that it prepared a survey containing four performance attributes that measure these interactions with customers:

■ The office staff is courteous.

■ Customer service personnel are responsive.

■ Employees keep their promises.

■ Billing problems are handled effectively.

The ratings for these four performance attributes can be added together to form a "humanistic interactions with customers index." This index should be a more consistent and reliable indicator of overall customer satisfaction with humanistic interactions than what could be obtained from any one performance attribute. The company might, for example, develop a profit-sharing compensation system based on changes in the index.

The following issues should be considered when developing a summed rating scale:

1. The items in a summed rating scale must be statements for which the customer is asked to give a rating. The items can-

not be yes–no questions or multiple-choice questions for which only one correct answer exists.

2. The fact that the performance attributes measure humanistic issues must be verified using a statistical technique such as factor analysis.

3. The consistency of the scale should be investigated using a set of procedures called *item analysis* (discussed in Spector's book *Summated Rating Scale Construction*).

Summing a set of performance attribute scores is not difficult. Questions concerning the reliability and validity of the new variable and the new rating scale, however, are quite complex. This subject is covered in detail by Spector.

Measurement scales for customer satisfaction research are often developed intuitively with little thought given to theoretical correctness. Summed rating scales and psychometric scales, however, must be statistically validated. In contrast to individual performance attribute questions, which are direct, summed ratings and psychometric questions are indirect. The object is not directly observable or measurable when indirect questions are used. For example, a customer can be asked directly if a shipment was delivered on time. Determining if a customer has high aspirations for his or her children is much more difficult.

Comparison Standards Other than Customer Expectations

It is commonly believed that satisfaction or dissatisfaction is predicted by comparing customer expectations with perceived performance. Dissatisfaction occurs if performance falls short of expectations. Satisfaction occurs if performance meets or exceeds expectations.

Recent research suggests that performance can be compared to standards other than expectations. Researchers point to inconsistencies in the logic that meeting or exceeding expectations necessarily results in satisfaction. Suppose, for example, that a customer purchased a product expecting poor performance. Actual poor performance, although meeting expectations, would most likely not generate satisfaction.

This argument is not purely academic. A consumer, for example, may purchase a substitute product if the preferred product is out of stock. A business executive, using a catalog to purchase office supplies, may consider the shipping charges and delivery time to be within expectations of mail-order or telephone purchases. The extra cost and added delay, however, may be unacceptable even if actual performance meets or exceeds expectations.

Spreng and Olshavsky suggest that comparing performance with customer desires, rather than expectations, will lead to a more accurate representation of customer satisfaction. Desires should be highly correlated with expectations. Separating the two concepts, however, will improve the questionnaire design. For example, the desire to not pay any shipping charges may be a more accurate determinant of satisfaction than the realization that shipping charges are about what was expected.

Actual performance of the product may be more important than initial expectations in determining satisfaction. Research by Churchill and Suprenant, for example, suggests that product performance of durable goods is a very important indicator of satisfaction.

A customer may also have opinions and perspectives that were not part of the original expectations. These new ideas can create both satisfaction and dissatisfaction. Satisfaction with high visibility and high-involvement products, such as automobiles, may be more dependent on performance than on expectations.

Woodruff, Cadotte, and Jenkins also suggest comparisons to standards of performance rather than expectations. They discuss "experience-based norms" that explicitly consider past experiences and beliefs about competing products and companies as well as the focal product. Therefore the focal product need not be the reference point for the comparisons.

Advertising claims and product publicity may also contribute to a norm based on experience. The distinction between expectations and norms can be clarified with the following example: Suppose that a customer was exposed to an advertising claim that he or she knew was not true. No expectation based on the advertising would be generated, since the claim was known to be false. The customer may still view the product with dissatisfaction because performance does not match the claim. False advertising, independent of realistic expectations, may create dissatisfaction.

Customers sometimes express expectations in terms of minimum performance standards. Rather than stating what performance should be or can be, the customer states what performance must be in order to continue purchasing from a supplier. Business requirements for "just-in-time" inventory are an example.

Customers may use other standards of comparison, not yet completely understood by researchers, to determine satisfaction. For example, customers sometimes mention comparisons to an "ideal" product, service, or company. Researchers are also investigating the concept of equity in determining satisfaction. Equity involves comparing and evaluating the benefits derived from a product or service relative to the benefits derived by other customers. Price and service appear to be key variables that customers use to determine satisfaction based on equity.

Tracking and estimating changes in customer satisfaction over time can be accomplished without an in-depth understanding of the comparison standards used by customers. The diagnostic value of the research, however, is dependent on insight into how customers make these comparisons. Changes that are designed and implemented without a full understanding of the customers' input may not lead to the desired results.

Customer satisfaction questionnaires often ask about satisfaction without stating or inquiring about the standard of comparison. This issue of comparison standards is still relevant since these questionnaires should be based on "Phase 1" input where the performance attributes were initially developed. The focus groups and open-ended responses typical of Phase 1 research are ideal for gaining an understanding of how customers make comparisons to determine satisfaction. Here are a few examples:

Comparing performance to desires:

> They are good but what I want is one company that can have all the products with high quality and reasonable prices.

What I would like is a salesperson at the department store that knows something, but maybe those days are gone.

Delivery time is what you would expect, but if it were faster I wouldn't have to keep so large an inventory.

I would like to see a sample so I could see the finished quality, but I expect that nobody really does that.

Satisfaction based on product performance other than expectations:

I wasn't interested in all those dials and buttons when I bought the VCR but now I use them and think that it is great.

The thing that has me sold on them is the excellent support service after the sale, and I didn't even know about that when I made the purchase.

Comparing performance to experience-based norms:

I form my opinions from stories I hear from other people.

In today's economy their price could be a lot worse.

They advertised great things but great things never happened.

Everything else is so high I know they are not overcharging.

Comparing performance to an ideal:

The service is all right but there must be better companies.

You want the best you can get—televisions that are going to last and don't cost a fortune.

Satisfaction based on an evaluation of equity:

I have traveled the whole country and I have seen what others are paying. We have reasonable rates here.

I know the richer patients get the best doctors and the poor people get the interns.

The personnel are not interested in working with older people.

Woodruff, Clemons, Schumann, Gardial and Burns, and Erevelles and Leavitt present overviews of some of the alternatives to expectations that have been used in customer satisfaction research. Advice concerning when to deviate from using expectations as the performance standard is difficult, because research on this subject is relatively new. Future research may indicate that customer satisfaction is a composite of various standards of performance with complex interactions among the standards.

Customer Involvement

Another area of current research concerns the relationship between satisfaction and the degree of customer involvement in selecting and using a product or service. Two major categories of involvement have been defined: situational involvement and enduring involvement.

Situational Involvement

Concern with a purchasing decision is an example of situational involvement. Customer involvement in the selection process is especially significant if the purchase encompasses a risk such as paying a high price. Durable goods are a typical example. Customer involvement can also be important in a wide variety of personal purchase decisions ranging from dinner wines to high fashion.

A key characteristic of situational involvement is the temporary nature of the involvement. For example, a consumer may spend a great deal of effort and time researching prices and performances of competing refrigerators. The involvement and interest in the refrigerator will decline rapidly although the refrigerator may be used every day for years.

Enduring Involvement

Enduring involvement is day-to-day involvement that is independent of the original purchase involvement. Products related to hobbies may evoke enduring involvement, but this type of involvement is rather rare.

Situational and enduring involvement are not completely defined by product categories. An automobile, for example, may create high enduring involvement with consumers interested in prestige and status but little enduring involvement with consumers interested in automobiles only as a method of transportation.

Researchers propose the following relationships between customer satisfaction and customer involvement:

High situational involvement generates:

- High performance expectations

- High initial satisfaction due to the extensive initial involvement and research

- A potential for dissatisfaction that increases over time as performance problems arise

- A higher sensitivity to actual performance

High enduring involvement generates:

- High but realistic performance expectations

- An ability to recognize and distinguish among various performance problems

- Greater awareness of performance problems

- Satisfaction that is highest for new products or for products owned for a very long time

- Satisfaction that is lower for products in the intermediate portion of the life cycle

Additional details concerning the relationship between customer involvement and customer satisfaction can be found in articles by Richins and Bloch, and by Bolfing and Woodruff.

Action Plan for Designing a Customer Satisfaction Questionnaire

An action plan for designing a customer satisfaction questionnaire consists of these steps:

1. Formulate the generic questionnaire.
   a. Develop the wording for the performance attributes.
   b. Select the competitors to be used for comparisons.
   c. Include demographic information.

2. Expand the questionnaire by adding enhancements.
   a. Incorporate open-ended questions.
   b. Include individual customer expectations and require-
      ments, if desired.
   c. Include feedback about specific customer problems, if
      appropriate.

3. Finalize the questionnaire.
   a. Develop an effective introduction.
   b. Decide on the balance between open- and closed-ended
      questions.
   c. Develop precise wording and measurement scales for
      every question.

8

Conducting the Customer Satisfaction Survey

Once the research customers have been identified, the critical performance attributes have been determined, and the basic design of the customer satisfaction survey has been established, several more decisions are necessary before the research can be conducted. Among the critical decisions is whether to conduct the survey with an in-house staff or to use a professional research organization. If the latter choice is made, an appropriate organization must be selected.

Decisions relating to sample size must be made. These are based on business and statistical requirements. The statistical decisions involve desired levels of confidence and acceptable margins of error. Comparisons among subgroups are almost always desired. The sample size must be large enough to produce valid comparisons among subgroups.

Adequate pretesting of the survey is very important. Problems with questionnaire wording and flow must be identified and corrected before beginning the major interviewing. If computer-assisted interviewing is used, computer programs must be debugged.

Quality control during interviewing and data analysis is critical. Training, supervision, and monitoring must receive the highest priority. Procedures must be in place to handle occasional negative reactions to the survey. Although the occurrences may be rare, customers who do not wish to participate must be deleted from the database for future interviews.

Selecting a Research Organization

Most companies choose a professional market research organization to both develop and conduct the customer satisfaction research. An outside organization adds objectivity and experience to the process. Proper administration of the research is also much more complex and difficult than simply hiring a few people "who like to talk and are good on the phone."

Telephone interviewers must work in a very structured and disciplined environment. The interviews must be standardized so that differences in demographics or geographic regions, for example, are attributed to differences in customer views rather than variation in interviewer styles. Outstanding customer service and telemarketing personnel are often mediocre research interviewers. The standardization discipline is frequently neither developed nor appreciated by telemarketers.

Not all researchers agree with the concept and merits of standardized interviewing. Jordan and Suchman, for example, note that standardization can inhibit clear communication between the interviewer and the respondent. Although this may be true in some situations, customer satisfaction research is based on comparing performance over time. This necessitates consistent interviewing that is not influenced by individual interviewers.

Outside research organizations range from large, prestigious, well-established companies to individuals operating from their basements or garages. The selection of a supplier should follow the same procedures used to choose other vendors. The successful supplier should:

- Demonstrate a thorough understanding of the project

- Describe a methodology that addresses all requirements and concerns

- Present evidence, based on background and experience, that the assignment will be successfully completed

- Offer a competitive price

Back-up, security, and confidentiality procedures and policies should be understood. Quality control in collecting and analyzing data must be apparent. One company, for example, discovered errors in excess of $10 million in the analysis of research data. The errors were traced to incorrect formulas in an undocumented spreadsheet model.

The references of potential suppliers should be checked, and the amount of subcontracting necessary to complete the project should be agreed upon. The interviewing facility should be visited. A few company personnel should attend a training session, thereby gaining an appreciation of the numerous details of successfully implementing the project. Monitoring a few telephone interviews provides an opportunity to better understand the customers and to assess the quality of the research organization.

Sample Size

The sample size required to produce a statistically valid sample is based on two judgment decisions:

Decision	Example
1. Margin of error	Accuracy is within $\pm 1\%$
2. Level of confidence	Sample is reliable with 95% confidence

Permissible margins of error and levels of confidence must be determined from the circumstances of the individual research project. For example, consider a product that requires a substantial capital investment but will succeed if purchased by a very small percentage of the potential market. The large capital investment requires a high level of confidence. A larger margin of error, however, might be acceptable because only a few customers are required. Conversely, research about a product that requires little initial investment but is very sensitive to market share will require a small margin of error, possibly at the expense of a lower level of confidence.

Table 8.1 presents the sample sizes necessary to satisfy various combinations of levels of confidence and margins of error. For a given confidence level, sample size decreases as the margin of error increases. For a fixed margin of error, sample size increases as the confidence level increases.

Several important points should be considered when using the information in Table 8.1:

1. The sample sizes are computed by considering only a single survey question. For example, a 95 percent level of confidence indicates that an error is likely about one time in 20. If a survey contains 20 questions, a very high probability exists that at least one of the questions will produce an answer outside the specified margin of error.

2. The level of confidence and the margin of error are computed for the entire sample. Individual cross-tabulations based on subsets of the sample will not achieve the same levels of confidence and margins of error.

3. The sample size computations are based on a generic question concerning estimation of percentages. These are only crude estimates when the research question involves something other than percentage estimation.

Table 8.1

Random Sample Sizes Required to Achieve Desired Levels of Confidence and Margins of Error

Margin	Level of Confidence							
of error	50%	75%	80%	85%	90%	95%	99%	99.9%
± 1.0%	1,140	3,307	4,096	5,184	6,766	9,604	16,590	19,741
± 2.0	285	827	1,024	1,296	1,692	2,401	4,148	4,936
± 3.0	127	358	456	576	752	1,068	1,844	2,194
± 4.0	72	207	256	324	423	601	1,037	1,234
± 5.0	46	133	164	208	271	385	664	790
± 7.5	21	59	73	93	121	171	296	351
± 10.0	12	34	41	52	68	97	166	198
± 15.0	6	15	19	24	31	43	74	88
± 20.0	3	9	11	13	17	25	42	50
± 50.0	2	2	2	3	3	4	7	10

Example: A random sample size of 752 is required to be 90% confident that the sample result is within 3% of the population value.

4. The computations assume that the sample was generated randomly from the population of interest. A truly random sample is very difficult to achieve. The company and research organization must cooperate in defining the population of interest and agreeing on the implementation specifications for the research.

5. The sample size computations measure only statistical sampling error. Many sources of error that are not of a statistical sampling nature can influence the accuracy and reliability of the results.

Students in introductory statistics courses often ask why a confidence level of 95 percent is tolerated when a 99 percent level can be achieved by increasing the sample size. The answer involves a somewhat formidable case of diminishing returns. For a selected margin of error, the sample size necessary to achieve a desired level of confidence becomes incrementally much larger for higher confidence levels. For example, the information in Table 8.1 can be used to illustrate the sample size changes required to increase confidence levels at a margin of error of ±1 percent:

Change in Level of Confidence	Additional Samples Required
75% to 80%	789
80% to 85%	1,088
85% to 90%	1,582
90% to 95%	2,838
95% to 99.5%	10,137

A sample size of 400 is often recommended to balance the need for reasonable levels of confidence and margins of error with the increased incremental requirement for additional samples. The following computations summarize what can be accomplished with a sample size of 400. The first set of computations indicates the margin of error associated with a specified level of confidence. The second set indicates the level of confidence associated with a specified margin of error.

Level of Confidence	Margin of Error
50%	±1.69%
75	±2.88
80	±3.20
85	±3.60
90	±4.11
95	±4.90
99	±6.44

For example, a sample size of 400 combined with a level of confidence of 85 percent will result in a margin of error of ±3.6 percent.

Margin of Error	Level of Confidence
±1%	31.1%
±2	57.6
±3	77.0
±4	89.0
±5	95.4
±6	98.4

For example, a sample size of 400 combined with a margin of error of ±4 percent will result in a level of confidence of 89 percent.

The total number of available customers must also be considered in the determination of an appropriate sample size. If a quarterly survey is to be conducted, for example, enough customers must be available so that any one customer is not contacted more frequently than about once each year.

Review of Potential Survey Errors

All marketing research projects are subject to a wide variety of possible errors. Potential sources of error should be reviewed before interviewing begins so that any remaining problems can be identified and rectified.

The potential sources of error discussed in this book are:

Sampling errors: These errors, governed by the laws of probability, occur because not every member of a population is included in a sample. Sample size computations, discussed in this chapter, are developed using probability and sampling error theory.

Coverage errors: These errors occur because the population was not defined correctly. Coverage errors are associated with the definition of customers, which is discussed in Chapter 3.

Nonresponse errors: These errors refer to the bias introduced because members of the sample were not included in the survey. This subject is discussed in Chapter 7.

Interviewer errors: These errors are created by interviewers who fail to follow instructions or to adequately probe open-ended questions. These errors are elaborated on in Chapter 7 and in this chapter.

Respondent errors: These errors arise when respondents give inaccurate information due to misunderstandings or loss of interest when participating in lengthy surveys. These errors are discussed in Chapter 7.

Questionnaire errors: These errors occur when the wording and order of questions affect the accuracy of the survey results. This subject is discussed in Chapter 7.

Administrative errors: These errors include data entry and analysis mistakes. They are discussed in this chapter.

Pretesting the Survey

Many of the potential problems with the wording and flow of questionnaires can be anticipated and corrected. There is no substitute, however, for actually conducting the interview or pretesting, with a limited number of customers before beginning full-scale research.

The specific objectives of a pretest are to:

Confirm that the questions achieve the desired objectives

Uncover wording that creates difficulties for the interviewer

Detect wording that is difficult for the respondent to understand or formulate a reply to

Isolate questions that do not capture the required information

Estimate the length of the interview

Estimate the response rate

The interpretation of a specific question can shift dramatically with small changes in wording. The attribute "has the lowest price," for example, produced a very low importance score on one set of pretests. Customers, however, mentioned price more often than any other attribute when responding to the open-ended question "What factors are most important in influencing your purchasing decision?" Although price was an important factor, absolute lowest price was not a requirement. The importance ratings dramatically increased when "has the lowest price" was changed to "has a competitive price."

Branching logic, which is used in many surveys, outlines the different paths through the questionnaire that are evoked depending on responses to previous questions. Any problems with questionnaire flow or branching logic must be identified during the pretest. This is also the time to isolate any programming errors, if computer-assisted interviewing is used.

The literature on pretesting is sparse. Converse and Presser, however, include an excellent chapter on pretesting.

The Interviewing Process

Planning and preparation are essential to effective research, but a successful survey also depends on how well the interviewing is implemented. Telephone surveys offer an outstanding opportunity to directly control the interviewing process. This potential opportunity, however, must be carefully administered.

Four key elements determine the success of a telephone-interviewing project: training, administrative procedures, monitoring, and quality control. The company should understand how these elements are implemented, whether the project is being conducted with an outside organization or with in-house personnel.

The training of interviewers can be handled in many different ways. New interviewers must be instructed in telephone techniques, made aware of the importance of standardization, and shown how to effectively handle open-ended questions. Training sessions for new and experienced interviewers should include:

- Discussion of the purpose of the study
- Performance standards for completed interviews and refusals
- Methods of handling refusals
- What is expected of open-ended question responses
- Procedure for callbacks
- Discussion of question branching logic
- Responses to questions typically asked by customers (for example, "How did you get my name?")
- Practice interviews with feedback from supervisors

Company personnel who attend training sessions should make a subjective assessment of the trainer's general knowledge and specific knowledge of the project. The trainer, for example, should discuss insights acquired during the pretesting process.

Administrative procedures include how the sample is selected, the procedures used for callbacks, and inspection of completed interviews with immediate feedback to interviewers.

Ongoing supervisor monitoring of samples of every interviewer's work is essential throughout the study. The supervisor should provide immediate feedback (both complimentary and corrective) in at least the following aspects of the interview:

- Quality of the introduction

- Effectiveness of probing techniques for open-ended questions

- Elimination of comments that might reinforce certain response patterns or otherwise bias the results

- Degree of standardization achieved

Procedures for quality control during the data collection and analysis phases must be established. Checks on data entry are essential. Computer-assisted interviewing can automate many of these procedures. For example, responses not within the defined permissible range can be instantaneously rejected. Consistency checks among answers to logically related questions can be performed.

Procedures for quality control should include maintaining a log (not available to the interviewer) that records every attempted call, the time interval between calls, and the time required to conduct each completed interview. These procedures will identify an interviewer who is falsifying entire interviews. If computer-assisted interviewing is not available, such procedures must be implemented manually.

Customer Reaction to the Satisfaction Survey

Most customers react favorably when asked to participate in satisfaction surveys. They appreciate the effort and realize that cooperation is in their best interest. Here are two examples:

They do an overall better job than the competitors. They have more interest in our business. They hire qualified people, such as yourself, to call us and show an interest in our business.

Service is not up to the same standard as their competitors. They have a certain touch of arrogance as if they are the only ones out there. I think this survey is a good thing if they pay attention to the results.

Procedures must be in place, however, to honor the desires of customers who do not wish to participate. In some firms, telephone surveys may be against company policy. Sometimes customers are extremely busy and react unfavorably. Occasionally, a customer may strongly object to a survey. For example, after completing a satisfaction survey, one customer told an interviewer:

I think this survey is in very poor taste, and I don't want you calling back for another one.

Customer satisfaction is easier to promise than to deliver. Customers who experience no improvement after cooperating with one satisfaction survey can be negative when recalled for another survey. Here are two actual comments:

They say they have a new attitude but everything is handled in the same old way—and it's lousy. You are wasting my time with this stuff.

They are kidding. They come in and tell us what we have to do and I don't think anything has changed. Don't call again unless there is really going to be a change.

Customers who ask not to be called again should be identified and removed from the list of potential respondents. Otherwise, antagonism and ill will are almost certain to be created—obviously running counter to the objective of a satisfaction survey. Computer-assisted interviewing offers an easy method to identify and record such customers: An interviewer can select a menu item on the computer screen to add the customer to a file of customers not to be recalled.

Formal complaints about surveys are rare. In business-to-business surveys, where the sponsoring company is identified, one research organization averages about one complaint in every 23,000 telephone calls.

Frequency of Surveys

Customer satisfaction studies are typically conducted either quarterly or annually. The following factors affect the frequency of surveys:

- Products at the beginning of a life cycle require frequent satisfaction evaluation.

- Established products or services require less frequent evaluations unless competitive conditions are rapidly changing.

- Customers making frequent buying decisions require more frequent evaluations.

- Profit sharing or bonus compensation tied to customer satisfaction requires frequent satisfaction evaluation.

Management consultant Tom Peters, in his book *Thriving on Chaos*, says that "formal customer satisfaction surveys every sixty to ninety days are a must." Although Peters does not use the same terminology, he seems to be suggesting an annual overall image satisfaction study and continual transaction-based satisfaction studies.

A related issue involves the point in the product life cycle at which satisfaction is measured. For example, at what point should the purchaser of a refrigerator or a set of bedroom furniture be interviewed regarding satisfaction with the product?

Decisions about the frequency of surveys should also consider how quickly the organization is responding to the previous survey results. Frequent surveys to monitor competition may be justified even if the organization has not yet responded to previous results. An individual customer, however, should not be interviewed a second time until some tangible responses to previous surveys have been implemented.

Action Plan for Conducting the Customer Satisfaction Research

1. Select the organization to conduct the research.
   a. Develop criteria for selecting a research organization (either in-house staff or a professional research firm).
   b. Solicit proposals.
   c. Evaluate proposals.
   d. Select a research organization.

2. Determine the required sample size.
   a. Consider the number of subgroup comparisons that are important to the research.
   b. Review desired levels of confidence and acceptable margins of error.

3. Review possible sources of error to be sure each is properly addressed.
   a. Sampling error
   b. Coverage error
   c. Nonresponse error
   d. Interviewer error
   e. Respondent error
   f. Questionnaire error
   g. Administrative error

4. Pretest the survey.
   a. Verify that the survey questions achieve the desired results.
   b. Detect wording that is difficult for the interviewer or customer.
   c. Estimate the length of the interview.
   d. Estimate the response rate.

     e. Verify that all computer programs are tested and working correctly.

5. Monitor quality control through the interviewing process.
     a. Evaluate interviewer training.
     b. Evaluate administrative methods: sample selection, procedures for callbacks, data entry validation, and analysis procedures.

9

Analyzing Results

Qualitative Research

A ppropriate analysis of survey results is critical to understanding the customers' perspectives and to developing strategies for improvement. A variety of techniques should be used to capture and analyze the important information generated during the research. For example, the analysis of qualitative research is discussed in this chapter. Techniques for analyzing percentages and proportions are covered in Chapter 10. Statistical methods are discussed in Chapter 11.

Different methodologies and techniques for analysis are introduced in each chapter. The techniques presented have all been successfully used to analyze customer satisfaction data. Some technical details, however, are omitted. Other techniques, not presented in these chapters, are undoubtedly in use to analyze survey results. Creative methods for analysis are limited only by the background and imagination of the analyst.

Each of the stages of customer satisfaction research requires an analysis of qualitative information:

1. The initial in-depth interviews and customer focus group transcripts must be analyzed to determine preliminary performance attributes.

2. The open-ended responses in mail or telephone surveys must be analyzed to determine the significance and importance of preliminary performance attributes.

3. The open-ended responses in mail or telephone surveys must be analyzed to measure customer satisfaction.

Guidelines and methodology for analyzing qualitative research are not standardized. Techniques range from subjective assessments to technically sophisticated analyses.

Impressive progress has been made in using computers to analyze qualitative information. Manipulation, summarization, and analysis of text information are now possible. Improvements in microcomputer technology are making content analysis and artificial-intelligence software both available and practical for the analysis of qualitative information.

In the foreseeable future, however, qualitative research will still be involved with subjective analyses and judgments. This chapter presents overviews of qualitative analysis as it exists today and of methodologies that are likely to improve analysis in the future.

Analysis of Open-Ended Responses

Identifying and extracting important themes, issues, and patterns from open-ended responses is called *coding*. An analyst studies specific responses and then develops more general or global categories to represent the comments. Coding is a data reduction technique similar in concept to the computation of means and standard deviations with quantitative data.

Here is an actual comment regarding dissatisfaction with a company's sales representatives:

The sales rep from _____ bought the guys chickens, bought lunch, and bought Cubs tickets. You guys won't do that.

Failure to purchase chickens or Cubs tickets may not be a major global problem. No provision for entertainment or gifts, however, could be a recurring theme. The coder might develop a preliminary code such as "failure to provide entertainment or gifts." Initial codes are refined and enhanced as more open-ended responses are analyzed.

Development of codes is highly subjective and dependent on the experience and background of the coder. One way to reduce subjectivity is to compare codes developed by two or more individuals acting independently. Differences in ideas can be examined and discussed, with the best ideas of each person being incorporated in a final set of codes.

Exhibit 9.1 presents a set of responses from a recent survey in which dissatisfaction with sales representatives was expressed. The comments are listed in a "key word in context" format. A computer program was used to search all open-ended responses for comments about sales reps. Sentences containing the key words *sales reps*, *sales rep*, or *rep* were located and printed. "Key word in context" is part of a set of procedures called *content analysis*. This methodology is discussed in more detail in the following section.

The reader is invited to study the responses in Exhibit 9.1 and to develop a set of preliminary codes to capture the main themes. Four experienced coders at a professional research firm undertook the same task; the results are presented in Exhibit 9.2.

The subjectivity associated with developing codes is illustrated by comparing the work of the four coders. Coder 4, for example, generated a very detailed set of codes. "Never" and "rarely" seeing a sales rep were included as separate categories. Coder 3 combined these thoughts into one code: "Sales reps do not keep in touch."

Exhibit 9.1

Responses to an Open-Ended Question about Sales Representatives

The SALES REP acts like I am not here.

The SALES REP is a klutz and thinks he can bullshit you with the weather and "let's go play golf" and does nothing to take care of the business you need.

We never see the SALES REP.

The SALES REP could not find a place to park, so he went back to the office.

The SALES REP did not have enough understanding about what we were doing to provide me with the program I could use.

I have never seen a SALES REP.

The SALES REP said she would come out and see us but that was over a year and a half ago.

The SALES REP dropped in one day without an appointment and would not leave—I honestly thought there'd be a fistfight.

Never met the SALES REP.

The SALES REP from _____ bought the guys chickens, bought lunch, and bought Cubs tickets. You guys won't do that.

The SALES REPS don't take you golfing like _____ does.

The SALES REP was not accommodating on the volume discounts.

I never see a SALES REP.

The SALES REP doesn't know anything.

The SALES REP's business card is seven years old, so that tells you what they think of us.

I don't feel the SALES REP knows his job.

The SALES REP never comes to my department to check on anything.

The SALES REP never gets in touch with me.

No SALES REP has been here to talk to me since July the 20th of 1984—that is not a very good impression.

We don't know the SALES REP.

The SALES REP is not willing to barter on discounts.

The SALES REP never calls on us.

Our SALES REP is the nicest guy, but he does not know anything.

The SALES REP lacks knowledge of the industry.

The SALES REPS are not interested in the needs of medium-sized companies.

We have called for a SALES REP at least ten times and no one shows up.

The SALES REP can't make decisions on his own, and we need answers right away.

I haven't seen a SALES REP in two years.

The SALES REP wouldn't even reschedule a meeting with me.

The SALES REP can't understand our problems.

I don't like the way the SALES REP comes across—too arrogant and demanding.

The SALES REP doesn't return calls, and that shows me that they don't want our business.

continued

I ask a question and my SALES REP never calls me back.

I never see the same SALES REP twice because they change so often.

The SALES REPS don't know anything.

I haven't seen a SALES REP in a long time.

The SALES REP doesn't consider my comments or suggestions important.

I've never talked to a SALES REP or seen one.

Four years ago the SALES REP said we were too small to deal with them.

The SALES REP is not professional—he actually solicited donations on our time.

The SALES REPS never give me any straight answers—I never get any answers.

The SALES REP would not cooperate regarding a problem—he wouldn't get back to me.

I have not seen a SALES REP in years—they don't even acknowledge that we exist.

The SALES REPS are unwilling to learn our requirements.

The SALES REP has only shown up once and he tried to tell me what to do, and that's not the way things work around here.

The SALES REP is just your basic arrogant salesman type.

We rarely ever see the SALES REP and that's good because he doesn't know what he is doing with price quotes anyway.

I have never talked to a SALES REP in the seven years I have been here.

My experience with the SALES REP is "Here is the policy—take it or leave it".

The SALES REP could care less about my problems—he never gets back to me.

I have never seen a SALES REP.

I haven't seen a SALES REP—if they came, they might get more business.

The SALES REP doesn't want to deal with us and we don't want to deal with them.

This is not one of the SALES REP's bigger accounts, and he doesn't care about it.

The SALES REPS do not know our side of the business.

I have never seen a SALES REP but am interested in talking with one—maybe you can figure out a way of getting one here.

I just have not seen a SALES REP at all. I have been here a year and I have not seen one.

I have not seen a SALES REP in God knows when.

The SALES REPS call me but never show up.

I get the attitude the SALES REPS don't feel we're that big a deal.

The SALES REPS don't make any sales calls, and your client used to be my favorite company.

The SALES REPS are rude and not courteous.

I don't think the SALES REP has a lot of knowledge.

The SALES REP thinks he's a big shot and won't give any personal attention.

The SALES REP is very pushy and just flies off the handle.

I wouldn't want their SALES REP around, according to what his manager said.

Exhibit 9.2

Preliminary Codes for Open-Ended Responses about Sales Representatives

Coder 1:	Sales reps won't entertain.
	Unwilling to negotiate rates and discounts.
	Lack of knowledge or experience.
	Never met or seen the sales rep.
	Lack of interest for the customer.
	Sales reps are unprofessional.
	Sales rep is pushy.
	Sales rep is unwilling to cooperate.
	Sales reps don't care to deal with customers.
	Other responses.
Coder 2:	Sales rep isn't knowledgeable/doesn't know his job.
	Sales rep doesn't know our company's business.
	Sales rep never calls on our business.
	Not familiar with the sales rep—never met.
	Sales rep calls but never shows up.
	Sales rep is arrogant/has a bad attitude.
	Sales rep exhibits unprofessional conduct.
	Sales rep doesn't negotiate reasonable discounts.
	Sales rep not interested in my business.
	The sales rep is unreasonable.
	The sales rep is uncooperative.
	Sales reps have high turnover.
	Other companies' reps offer incentives or gifts.
	Other responses.
Coder 3:	Sales reps not interested in customer.
	Sales reps not professional.
	Sales reps not responsive.
	Sales reps not competent.
	Sales reps do not keep in touch.
	Sales reps can't get discounts.
	Difficulties with sales rep turnover.
	Competitor reps offer incentives.

continued

> *Coder 4:* We never see a sales rep.
> We haven't seen a rep for a while/rarely see the rep.
> Rep is not knowledgeable—general.
> Rep is not knowledgeable about our industry.
> Unwilling to give discounts.
> Does not supply adequate perks.
> Dislike rep's personality traits.
> Rep ignores company because not large account.
> Rep does not return calls/get back to us.
> Rep does not care about my problems.
> Unprofessional sales behavior.
> Rep does not give us answers.
> Other responses.

Coder 4 created separate categories for "Rep is not knowledgeable—general" and "Rep is not knowledgeable about our industry." Coder 1 combined these thoughts into "Lack of knowledge or experience." Coder 2 created codes for "Sales rep isn't knowledgeable/doesn't know his job" and "Sales rep doesn't know our company's business." Coder 3 combined all the thoughts (and several others) into "Sales reps not competent."

Coder 2 probably generated the most descriptive headings. The coder's background included writing for a local newspaper and experience in writing attention-getting headlines. Coder 1 was the least experienced of the four coders and created the longest list of "Other responses."

Coder 3 did not include an "Other responses" category but nevertheless generated the smallest number of total codes. All of the other coders placed the comment "I wouldn't want their sales rep around, according to what his manager said" in the "Other responses" classification. Coder 3 placed this comment in the "Sales reps not professional" category (although there is no indication of what the manager actually said). This is another example of where an interviewer probe would have been helpful.

All of the coders established a category for failure to provide gifts and incentives, but their descriptive titles varied:

- Sales reps won't entertain.

- Other companies' reps offer incentives or gifts.

- Competitor reps offer incentives.

- Does not supply adequate perks.

Note that two of the coders focused on the company's actions, whereas the other two focused on actions by competitors.

A code for high turnover of sales reps was created by Coders 2 and 3 but not by the other two. Coder 1 created a code for "Sales rep is pushy," but the other three coders placed this comment in other categories.

Comparing the work of several coders is beneficial, because the best ideas of all the coders can be incorporated in a final set of codes. Even after codes are established, different analysts may place open-ended responses in different categories. Thus the establishment of codes and the coding process both contribute to inconsistencies in the final results.

The subject of coder consistency is discussed by Hughes and Garrett and by Kalton and Stowell. The innovative computer techniques introduced later in this chapter may eventually help increase the consistency and reliability of the coding process.

Content Analysis

Content analysis is a set of techniques that examine and analyze information represented as text. Applications to customer satisfaction research include the analysis of focus group transcripts, in-depth interviews, and open-ended questions.

One way to "quantify" qualitative information is to count the number of occurrences of a specific idea, thought, or observation. The number of times a specific word appears in a transcript is an ideal example. This counting of occurrences is called *word frequency analysis*.

Word frequency analysis is used to determine patterns of usage levels for words. Uninteresting words (such as *a*, *the*, *is*, *of*, or *was*) can be routinely eliminated. The number of times a word occurs is valuable input in the development of preliminary codes from open-ended responses or preliminary themes from focus group sessions.

Computer software is available to perform word frequency counts. Sophisticated software can recognize the similarity of word forms (*consumer* and *consumers*, for example) and can handle prefixes and suffixes.

One drawback to word frequency counts, however, is that they do not provide information about how the word is being used. This is especially troublesome when words have multiple meanings. Difficulties also occur when the intent of the word usage is not known. For example, *quality products* and *reasonable price* are associated with both companies in the following survey comments:

> Company A provides quality products at a reasonable price.

> Company B certainly doesn't make quality products and, as for a reasonable price, well, that's a joke.

Word frequencies must be combined with indications of how the words were intended to be used. This can be accomplished using key-word-in-context capabilities. The objective of this technique is to list all of the sentences that include a key word or phrase. Exhibit 9.1 is an example of a key word in context application.

Associations among words can also be represented and manipulated mathematically. These applications are discussed in the following section.

Weber offers an excellent introduction to content analysis.

Artificial-Intelligence Techniques

Artificial intelligence uses computer hardware and software to perform activities that would be considered intelligent if the same activities were performed by human beings. Artificial-intelligence techniques encompass several different methodologies and disciplines.

The development of expert systems is one branch of artificial intelligence. An expert system captures knowledge about how a human expert solves a specific problem. The information, rules, and procedures necessary to solve the problem are constructed by an individual trained in obtaining this type of data. Computer software is then used to solve the problem using the same information, rules, and procedures.

A successful expert system application will disseminate the human expert's knowledge to other members of the organization. Expert systems are also excellent tools for training employees.

Expert systems have been developed to help in coding open-ended responses. One expert system for coding is described by Carley. Coding is accomplished in two stages. In the first stage, a coder codes the questions in the usual manner. In the second stage, the expert system analyzes the completed codes for inconsistencies and problems. The expert system helps achieve standardization and consistency in the coding process.

Because expert systems are a relatively new technology, their use for coding is not widespread. A better appreciation of the applicability of expert systems to coding open-ended responses will be gained as more applications are developed.

Another exciting branch of artificial intelligence involves "neural network" technology. This software is optimized for analyzing text data. The computer program conducts a mathematical cluster analysis on words that tend to be associated with each other. The program identifies the patterns of similarity among important words. This software is in various experimental stages and is likely to become very practical in the next few years.

Subjectivity in the Analysis of Qualitative Research

A great deal of subjectivity is used in analyzing the results of qualitative research. The quality and comprehensiveness of codes developed to analyze open-ended responses, for example, are dependent on the experience and intelligence of the coder. Differences in the skills of coders can change the interpretation of survey results.

Computer analysis of qualitative information, using techniques based on mathematics and artificial-intelligence, promises to provide additional insights and perspectives while reducing reliance on subjectivity. The development and implementation of these techniques, however, are still in very experimental stages.

10

Analyzing Results

Percentages and Proportions

D ata analysis is the transformation of raw data into a form that will make these data easy to understand and to interpret. It is the rearranging, ordering, and manipulation of data to provide descriptive information. Describing responses or observations is usually the initial stage of analysis.

Data analysis can range from examining percentage changes to applying sophisticated statistical techniques. The reasons for the analysis and the interests of the intended audience both play an important part in selecting the analysis method. The techniques used for management reporting, for example, are different from those used to analyze survey reliability and validity.

Two approaches that employ relatively unsophisticated statistical analyses are:

1. Our reference average is 4.215 with a standard deviation of 1.048. Since the sample size is 500, the standard error is 0.0469. This indicates that an increase to 4.307 is statistically significant at the 95 percent confidence level. Therefore, an increase from 4.215 to 4.307 or greater can be reasonably attributed to real improvement rather than sampling variability.

2. Thirty percent of our customers gave us a very favorable rating on overall satisfaction, and 4 percent gave us a very unfavorable rating. Our goal is to increase the very favorable percentage and reduce the very unfavorable percentage.

Most audiences will have little difficulty understanding goals that involve increasing the percentage of very satisfied customers. The statistical significance of an increase in average rating from 4.215 to 4.307, on the other hand, may be much more difficult to comprehend.

Reporting the results of advanced statistical techniques such as factor analysis or discriminate analysis is even more difficult. These analyses, however, are important in developing a technical understanding of customer satisfaction. The techniques and reports, therefore, must be carefully geared to the intended audience.

The data analysis techniques discussed in this and the next chapter range from simple percentages to more advanced techniques such as correlation and factor analysis. The techniques are summarized in Exhibit 10.1.

Not every analysis technique is appropriate for every circumstance. Conversely, many creative analyses can be developed that are not discussed in these chapters. The information in these chapters, however, will provide a good background for understanding the variety of analysis techniques available.

Descriptive Percentages

In analysis of customer satisfaction data, one very important statistic is the percentage of customers who give an excellent rating to every general satisfaction question. These questions include

---

Exhibit 10.1

Customer Satisfaction
Data Analysis Techniques

Percentages
Percentage of respondents who rated the client excellent on all of the overall satisfaction ratings

Percentage of customers who never gave the company a dissatisfaction rating on any of the performance attributes

Percentage of very dissatisfied customers

"Penalty–reward" analysis

Relatively Simple Statistics
Averages, standard deviations, and statistical significance of trends

Gap between customer expectations and performance

More Complex Statistical Techniques
Correlation analysis

Multiple regression analysis

Discriminant analysis

Factor analysis

Correspondence analysis

Conjoint analysis

---

those relating to overall satisfaction, to recommending the company, and to intent to use the company again. A typical score for excellent ratings on all three types of questions is 30 percent.

Combining "excellent" and "very good" ratings when reporting percentages is usually not a good idea. The combination generally represents a large percentage of the total responses (typically at least 70 percent). Although large percentages of satisfied customers are certainly welcome, the combined percentage is not sensitive to critical shifts from "very good" to "excellent" or vice versa.

Descriptive proportions should be calculated for every combination of performance attribute and company. This information helps put in proper perspective the strengths and weaknesses of the sponsoring company and its major competitors.

Descriptive percentages can be used in the following three types of trend analyses to provide additional insights, especially if the data are collected quarterly:

1. Plots of percentages over time to indicate where improvements have been accomplished and where additional emphasis is necessary

2. Statistical procedures to determine if significant changes have occurred from the previous period

3. Statistical quality control limits to highlight areas where significant trends are occurring

The statistical manipulation of percentages is presented in most introductory statistics texts. Calculations of control limits are described in Grant and Leavenworth and in other books on statistical quality control. An initial drawback to statistical control charts is that a reasonable amount of past history must be available before the control limits can be established.

Penalty–Reward Analysis

A penalty–reward analysis divides customer requirements into three categories:

1. A *basic factor* creates dissatisfaction when not achieved but does not increase satisfaction when achieved or exceeded. Thus a penalty is incurred for not meeting the requirement, but no reward is gained for meeting or exceeding the requirement. A clerk making correct change is an example of a basic factor.

2. A *performance factor* results in a reward when the requirement is exceeded and in a penalty when the requirement is not satisfied. Most customer requirements are in this category.

3. An *excitement factor* incurs no penalty if not achieved but adds value if the requirement is exceeded. Here are a few examples of attributes that are excitement factors:
   a. A bank teller who addresses customers by name as they approach the teller window.
   b. Free admission to the Cleveland Museum of Art.
   c. Excellent food on an airline.

Attributes are classified into basic, performance, and excitement factors by using the following three-step procedure (a rating of 5 indicates a high level of satisfaction and a rating of 1 indicates a low level of satisfaction):

1. Interpret the ratings as follows: A rating of 1 or 2 is defined as deficient, a rating of 3 or 4 is defined as meeting requirements, and a rating of 5 is defined as exceeding requirements.

2. Consider the customers who rated a specific performance attribute as deficient (1 or 2). Compute the percentage of those customers who also rated the company 5 on overall satisfaction. Compute similar percentages for the meets-requirements (3 or 4) and exceeds-requirements (5) categories. For example, suppose that 76 customers rate "Billing is accurate" either a 1 or a 2. Of these 76 customers, 4 gave the company a 5 rating on overall satisfaction. The corresponding percentage calculation is $4/76 = .0526$ (5.26 percent).

3. Apply the following definitions:
   Basic: Meets and exceeds percentages are not statistically different, but the deficient percentage is statistically different from the other two.

   Performance: Deficient, meets, and exceeds percentages are all statistically different.

   Excitement: Deficient and meets percentages are not statistically different, but the exceeds percentage is statistically different from the other two.

Here are a few examples from a recent survey:

Example 1: A Basic Factor
Rating on Individual Performance Attribute

	1–2 Deficiency	3–4 Meets	5 Exceeds
"Billing is accurate."	5.26%	52.06%	50.67%

Only 5.26 percent of the customers who rated accurate billing as a deficiency also gave the company an excellent overall satisfaction rating. This is significantly smaller than the percentage of customers who rated billing accuracy as either meeting or exceeding requirements and who also rated overall satisfaction as excellent.

The percentages in the meets and exceeds categories are not significantly different. This implies that no reward is given for exceeding the requirement but a penalty is incurred if the requirement is not met. This is a basic factor.

Example 2: A Performance Factor
Rating on Individual Performance Attribute

	1–2 Deficiency	3–4 Meets	5 Exceeds
"Is quick to respond to questions."	3.36%	17.00%	73.49%

The deficiency, meets, and exceeds categories are all statistically different for this attitude. This is a performance factor. The company will be rewarded if expectations are exceeded and will also incur a penalty if expectations are not met.

Example 3: An Excitement Factor
Rating on Individual Performance Attribute

	1–2 Deficiency	3–4 Meets	5 Exceeds
"Is willing to adjust to individual customer requirements."	7.26%	8.88%	58.27%

This attribute is an excitement factor. No penalty is incurred if expectations are not met (since 7.26 percent and 8.88 percent are not statistically different). The company, however, will be rewarded if expectations are exceeded. Another possibility is that none of the categories—deficiency, meets, or exceeds—is statistically different. In this case, the performance attribute is probably not related to customer satisfaction.

The classification of attitudes as basic, performance, and excitement factors will change over time. For example, a knowledgeable sales clerk in a department store might be viewed as an excitement factor today, but 40 years ago this would most likely have been a basic factor. A computerized system for tracking shipments is a business example of an attribute that may be an excitement factor today but will be a basic factor in the next five to ten years.

Penalty–reward analyses provide valuable insights into the attributes that excite customers. Satisfaction ratings for performance and excitement factors will improve as more customers perceive the company as exceeding requirements.

Brandt provides a more detailed discussion of the penalty–reward analysis model.

Gap Analysis: Expectations vs. Performance

A gap often exists between the expectations and requirements of customers and the performance of a company. A procedure called *gap analysis* is used to identify where these shortcomings occur. This analysis is useful in developing strategic and tactical plans for performance improvement.

A gap analysis requires a survey structure similar to that in the two examples presented in the "Individual Customer Expectations and Requirements" section of Chapter 7. The first format (page 84) was used to obtain information about the importance and the satisfaction of each performance attribute. The objective is to match or exceed customer expectations. This is accomplished by determining where significant gaps occur between importance and satisfaction.

For example, suppose that a sample of 400 customers produced the following number of observations in each importance/satisfaction category:

Attribute: Ease of reaching a customer service representative

		Satisfaction					
		1	2	3	4	5	Total
	1	3	2	4	5	3	17
	2	10	6	6	2	2	26
Importance	3	13	14	5	6	1	39
	4	43	22	10	3	0	78
	5	138	34	28	32	8	240

The table indicates that the ease of reaching a customer service representative is very important: 240 of the 400 customers (60 percent) associated the highest importance rating with this attribute. However, 138 of those 240 customers (57.5 percent) gave the attribute the lowest possible satisfaction rating. This performance attribute requires immediate attention. The gap between high importance and low satisfaction must be rectified.

The corresponding data for another attribute yields a different perspective, as shown below:

Attribute: Quality of information booklets

		Satisfaction					
		1	2	3	4	5	Total
	1	0	0	32	44	77	153
	2	0	1	14	30	67	112
Importance	3	1	3	27	20	37	88
	4	1	2	5	5	14	27
	5	2	1	3	4	10	20

In this case, 153 customers rated the attribute as very unimportant. However, 77 of these 153 customers (50 percent) were extremely satisfied with company performance in this area. A high degree of satisfaction is therefore associated with an attribute that is relatively unimportant from the customer's perspective.

Results of gap analyses are often presented in a two-dimensional grid:

		Satisfaction	
		Low	High
Importance	**Low**	Low priority	Unnecessary strengths—possible overkill
	High	Attributes that need attention—area where priorities should be focused	Current company strengths

The "Ease of reaching a customer service representative" attribute is classified in the high-importance/low-satisfaction section, while the "Quality of information booklets" attribute is placed in the low-importance/high-satisfaction area.

The assignment of attributes in the two-dimensional grid can be quantified by plotting the pairs of points associated with the average-importance and average-satisfaction rating for each performance attribute. For example, using a scale from 1 to 5, where 5 is either very important or very satisfied, the performance attributes can be assigned to the grid as follows:

1. *Low priority:* average importance and average satisfaction ratings both under 3.00

2. *Attributes that need attention:* average importance ratings greater than 3.00 and average satisfaction ratings less than 3.00

3. *Overkill areas:* average importance ratings less than 3.00 and average satisfaction ratings greater than 3.00

4. *Current company strengths:* average importance and average satisfaction ratings both greater than 3.00

Caution must be exercised in plotting average values because important individual differences may be masked when averages are used.

The second example in Chapter 7 (page 85) used a structure in which a requirement defined by a customer was paired with a rating of satisfaction. The pairs of responses can be arranged for analysis as shown below:

		Performance					
		a	b	c	d	e	Total
	a	15	2	11	3	5	36
	b	3	12	8	7	3	33
REQUIREMENT	c	4	4	18	12	9	47
	d	6	4	3	23	6	42
	e	1	2	4	4	15	26
	Total	29	24	44	49	38	184

Customers whose requirements are satisfied appear on the diagonal of the table. For example, the 18 customers represented by the intersection of Row c and Column c are customers who require price information within one to two hours and who obtain the information in a one to two-hour period.

Numbers to the left of a diagonal in any row represent customers whose requirements are exceeded. For example, 8 customers in Row c (4 in Column a and 4 in Column b) received information in less than the one- to two-hour requirement. Numbers to the right of a diagonal represent customers whose requirements are not satisfied.

For each requirement, the percentage of customers whose requirements were not satisfied, satisfied, and exceeded can be calculated:

	Percentage Not Satisfied	Percentage Satisfied	Percentage Exceeded
Immediately	58%	42%	0%
Within one hour	55	36	9
Within one to two hours	45	38	17
Within three to four hours	14	55	31
More than four hours	0	58	42

As expected, the percentage of customers whose requirement is not satisfied declines as the requirement becomes less demanding. A large difference in the not-satisfied percentage exists between the one- to two-hour requirement (45 percent) and the three- to four-hour requirement (14 percent). The company does a good job of responding within three to four hours and could improve satisfaction substantially if that time could be reduced by one to two hours.

Effective Tools for Analysis and Reporting

Percentages and proportions should be an integral part of the analysis and reporting of customer satisfaction survey results. They are easy to understand and interpret and provide unique insights. A penalty–reward analysis, for example, can pinpoint the performance attributes that excite customers. Analysis of gaps highlight critical areas where improvement is required.

11

Analyzing Results

Statistical Techniques

S tatistical techniques help discover complex relationships among satisfaction ratings and various performance attributes. Recently developed techniques that emphasize graphical and pictorial output facilitate visualization and understanding.

The first technique to be discussed—the arithmetic average—is a statistic that is almost always reported in customer satisfaction research. Five other statistical techniques—correlation analysis, multiple regression, discriminant analysis, factor analysis, and correspondence analysis—will also be discussed.

All of the statistical techniques will be illustrated using a single set of data. The research subject is customer satisfaction with three suppliers of polyvinyl chloride resin. This very competitive industry had experienced reduced demand in 1991 because of weak economic conditions. Profit margins had eroded due to decreased demand, price reductions, and excess production capacity.

Although some customers require production to exacting specifications, the resin is regarded as a "commodity" product for many applications. Price and delivery time are the primary performance requirements in these situations, because quality is perceived as equal among the suppliers. Customer satisfaction in commodity-product industries is critical. Small differences in satisfaction can translate into substantial changes in sales due to the competitive nature of the business.

Manufacturers of residential and commercial pipe were targeted for the customer satisfaction research. Polyvinyl chloride resin is used to manufacture pipe for new home construction. The resin competes favorably with copper and iron because of its lower weight and cost. It is also used in commercial construction for the same reasons.

Cities and other municipalities purchase polyvinyl chloride pipe for water systems, storm drains, and sanitary sewers. Easier installation, due to its lower weight, makes this type of pipe more attractive than concrete or ductile iron alternatives. The pipe is also used in irrigation systems because it flexes to accommodate soil expansion and contraction. Other applications include sprinkler systems, marine and offshore systems, heat pumps, gasket pipe, telephone conduit, and fiber optic duct.

The resin is considered a commodity product for these applications. The major quality issue is the amount of contamination in the resin. Contamination occurs when foreign substances, such as metal particles, are introduced into the resin.

The customer satisfaction survey includes an overall satisfaction score and ratings for 13 performance attributes for three firms—Plastic Polymers Inc. and two major competitors, PVC Resins Inc. and the Industrial Chemical Company.

Computer-assisted interviewing technology was used to randomize the order of inquiring about the following 13 performance attributes:

■ Questions are answered quickly.

■ Price is competitive.

- Problems are handled effectively.
- Office staff is courteous.
- Just-in-time delivery schedules are met.
- Warranty claims are handled promptly.
- Shipments are delivered to specifications.
- Technical support personnel are knowledgeable.
- Billing is accurate.
- Customer requirements drive the company.
- Customer service personnel are responsive.
- Resin is not contaminated.
- The company is professional in business dealings.

The attributes were rated using a scale ranging from 1 (very unfavorable) to 5 (very favorable). The data consisted of 7,223 completed telephone interviews.

Arithmetic Averages

The arithmetic average is commonly used to analyze customer satisfaction data. Comparing arithmetic averages is an easy way to answer two important questions:

1. *How do scores for various performance attributes differ at one particular point in time?* For example, the arithmetic averages for Plastic Polymers' performance attributes in the fourth quarter of 1991 were:

4.460	Office staff is courteous.
4.414	Customer service personnel are responsive.
4.362	Technical support personnel are knowledgeable.
4.360	Shipments are delivered to specifications.
4.314	Billing is accurate.
4.286	The company is professional in business dealings.
4.205	Customer requirements drive the company.
4.202	OVERALL SATISFACTION

4.200   Resin is not contaminated.
4.193   Problems are handled effectively.
4.186   Questions are answered quickly.
4.156   Just-in-time delivery schedules are met.
4.041   Warranty claims are handled promptly.
3.995   Price is competitive.

Seven performance attribute averages registered greater scores than the overall satisfaction average, while six attributes were below the overall average. Office, customer service, and technical staffs are company strengths. On the other hand, customers viewed pricing policies much less favorably. Handling warranty claims and meeting delivery schedules were also among the lower average scores.

These averages must be compared with the competitors' scores to more clearly define company strengths and weaknesses. For example, although the office staff received a high rating, it is possible that a competitor's office staff received an even higher rating.

2. *How are scores for the same performance attribute changing over time?* For example, Plastic Polymers' average scores for "Resin is not contaminated" during eight consecutive quarters were:

1990	Quarter 1	3.899
	Quarter 2	4.002
	Quarter 3	4.133
	Quarter 4	4.029
1991	Quarter 1	4.168
	Quarter 2	4.173
	Quarter 3	4.198
	Quarter 4	4.200

The average score increased from 3.899 to 4.200 in eight quarters. Seven of the eight quarters showed an improvement over the previous quarter.

Statistical significance tests should be used to provide more rigorous answers to both of these questions about averages. For example, for the second question, a significance test can determine if the increase in the 1991 scores for "Resin is not contaminated" (from 4.168 to 4.200) is most likely a true indicator of progress or just a statistical fluke due to sampling error. Appropriate significance tests are covered in nearly all elementary statistics texts.

Although helpful, averages do not provide explicit insights into how overall satisfaction can be improved. Improvements in the lowest average score ("Price is competitive") may not improve overall satisfaction as much as improvement in some of the other attributes (such as answering questions quickly or handling problems effectively).

Examining how individual ratings are concentrated about the arithmetic mean will usually provide additional insights. For example, consider how the ratings for the performance attribute "Just-in-time delivery schedules are met" are disbursed about the arithmetic average of 4.156:

	Rating	Number of Responses
Very unfavorable	1	1,036
	2	118
	3	284
	4	599
Very favorable	5	4,672
	Total	6,709

Eliminated from the calculation of the arithmetic average were 514 responses of "Don't know."

This performance attribute satisfies customer expectations in the vast majority of cases but occasionally suffers serious breakdowns. Further insight can be gained by examining the demographic characteristics of the customers who gave a very unfavorable rating to the just-in-time delivery attribute. In this case, the problem was isolated to one geographic division. The difficulty was rectified with a change in operating procedures and the addition of another dispatcher.

The arithmetic average can be very deceptive. There is no guarantee that about half the observations are above the arithmetic average and half are below. Unfortunately, many individuals interpret the arithmetic average in this manner.

Many researchers argue that measurement scales based on ratings are not refined enough to support calculation of arithmetic averages. Even if the computation is justifiable, the practical impact of an average increasing from 4.113 to 4.202 may be difficult to interpret.

The biggest drawback to the use of an arithmetic average, however, is that it is relatively boring to many people. Percentages and graphs create more excitement. Nevertheless, the arithmetic average has become standard in customer satisfaction reporting because of its apparent simplicity.

Correlation Analysis

Correlation analysis is used to determine the performance attributes that have the greatest influence on overall satisfaction. Calculating a correlation coefficient is routine in most statistical analysis software packages.

The correlation coefficient is a number between ± 1 that indicates the degree of linear association between two variables. Large numerical values suggest strong association. A correlation coefficient of $+1$ indicates perfect positive correlation. A correlation coefficient near zero implies little linear relationship between the variables.

A negative correlation indicates that overall satisfaction declines as one of the performance attribute ratings increases. Although important in other analyses, negative correlation coefficients should not occur between overall satisfaction and individual performance attributes.

The correlation coefficients between the overall satisfaction rating and the individual performance attributes for Plastic Polymers are presented in Table 11.1. An examination of these corre-

---

Table 11.1

**Correlation Coefficients between Overall Satisfaction
Rating and Individual Performance Attributes:
Plastic Polymers Inc.**

.74422	Questions are answered quickly.
.72204	The company is professional in business dealings.
.72021	Problems are handled effectively.
.67265	Just-in-time delivery schedules are met.
.63207	Customer requirements drive the company.
.56994	Shipments are delivered to specifications.
.58188	Office staff is courteous.
.59036	Customer service personnel are responsive.
.58137	Resin is not contaminated.
.53310	Price is competitive.
.51827	Technical support personnel are knowledgeable.
.50155	Warranty claims are handled promptly.
.49531	Billing is accurate.

---

lation coefficients indicates that performance attributes involving human interactions tend to be highly correlated with overall satisfaction. For example:

.74422 Questions are answered quickly.
.72204 The company is professional in business dealings.
.72021 Problems are handled effectively.
.63207 Customer requirements drive the company.

Performance attributes with lower correlations are more related to mechanical or "systems" aspects (e.g., "Billing is accurate") than to human interactions.

Correlation analysis does not prove that a cause-and-effect relationship exists. Improvements in the human-interaction attributes, however, should have the greatest impact on the overall satisfaction rating.

Passive performance attributes that do not measure specific actionable characteristics are often highly correlated with overall satisfaction. This occurs not because improvements relating to the attribute will improve overall satisfaction, but because the attribute is really just another measure of overall satisfaction. For example, the attribute "The company is reliable in business dealings" is more a measure of overall satisfaction than an attribute for which specific actions for improvement can be implemented.

A pretest of the survey will often identify passive attributes. For example, an open-ended question asking why the customer perceives the company to be reliable (or unreliable) in business dealings would probably generate responses in which the customer describes strong or weak characteristics of other performance attributes:

> The company is not reliable in business dealings because the billing is never accurate.

> The company is reliable because the product quality is always excellent.

The attribute "The company is reliable in business dealings" should be eliminated from the survey because the information is already being captured in other performance attributes (i.e., billing and product quality).

Note that although "Questions are answered quickly" is most correlated with overall satisfaction, the attribute ranked only tenth in average score among the 13 attributes. Improving performance in this category, therefore, should be a high priority for Plastic Polymers.

Multiple Regression

Multiple regression is a statistical technique used to develop an equation in which the customers' ratings of the performance attributes are used to predict the overall satisfaction rating. Multiple regression helps in understanding the importance and predictive accuracy of the performance attributes. The technique is therefore especially useful during the initial selection of performance attributes.

The Multiple Regression Equation

The multiple regression equation for the overall satisfaction rating for Plastic Polymers is:

$$Y = 0.38084 + 0.19326X_1 + 0.01465X_2 + 0.16150X_3 + 0.07234X_4 + 0.13375X_5 - 0.04712X_6 + 0.07151X_7 - 0.01309X_8 - 0.04526X_9 + 0.04959X_{10} - 0.01581X_{11} + 0.08538X_{12} + 0.21507X_{13}$$

where:

Y = Overall satisfaction rating

X_1 = Questions are answered quickly
X_2 = Price is competitive
X_3 = Problems are handled effectively
X_4 = Office staff is courteous
X_5 = Just-in-time delivery schedules are met
X_6 = Warranty claims are handled promptly
X_7 = Shipments are delivered to specifications
X_8 = Technical support personnel are knowledgeable
X_9 = Billing is accurate
X_{10} = Customer requirements drive the company
X_{11} = Customer service personnel are responsive
X_{12} = Resin is not contaminated
X_{13} = The company is professional in business dealings

For example, suppose that a customer gave the following ratings for the 13 performance attributes:

Rating	Performance Attribute
3	Questions are answered quickly.
4	Price is competitive.
4	Problems are handled effectively.
3	Office staff is courteous.
4	Just-in-time delivery schedules are met.
3	Warranty claims are handled promptly.
3	Shipments are delivered to specifications.
3	Technical support personnel are knowledgeable.
4	Billing is accurate.
4	Customer requirements drive the company.
3	Customer service personnel are responsive.
3	Resin is not contaminated.
4	The company is professional in business dealings.

These ratings are entered in the equation to produce the following prediction of overall satisfaction:

$$
\begin{aligned}
Y &= 0.38084 + 0.19326(3) + 0.01465(4) + 0.16150(4) + \\
&\quad 0.07234(3) + 0.13375(4) - 0.04712(3) + 0.07151(3) - \\
&\quad 0.01309(3) - 0.04526(4) + 0.04959(4) - 0.01581(3) + \\
&\quad 0.08538(3) + 0.21507(4) \\
&= 3.53745
\end{aligned}
$$

In any one survey, the overall satisfaction will be an integer (a rating of either 1, 2, 3, 4, or 5). The equation above, however, indicates that the average value of all overall satisfaction ratings for surveys with that particular combination of performance ratings will be 3.53745. An average rating near 3.5 is very reasonable, since about half of the individual performance attributes were rated 3 while the other half were rated 4.

Analyzing Predictive Accuracy

The multiple regression equation was developed with survey data from the third quarter of 1991. Predictive accuracy was then analyzed using data from the fourth quarter. This procedure is necessary so that the information used to develop the multiple regression equation is not the same information applied to assessing the equation's accuracy.

The overall predictive accuracy of the multiple regression equation can be analyzed using Table 11.2. The predicted overall satisfaction rating in the table was computed by rounding the rating generated by the equation.

Predictive accuracy can be viewed from two different perspectives. The second column in the table, for example, indicates that the multiple regression equation predicted 12 questionnaires would receive the lowest overall satisfaction score (a rating equal to one). The remaining columns indicate the actual overall satisfaction ratings associated with these 12 questionnaires. In other words, 11 of the 12 questionnaires actually received a rating of 1, and the twelfth survey registered a rating of 2.

At the other extreme, the equation predicted 2,616 questionnaires would receive the highest possible score. This was correct for 1,987 of the cases. Another 516 of the questionnaires re-

Table 11.2

Overall Predictive Accuracy of the Multiple Regression Equation

Predicted Overall Satisfaction		Actual Overall Satisfaction Rating					
Rating	Number	1	2	3	4	5	6[a]
1	12	11	1	0	0	0	0
2	148	53	56	31	5	2	1
3	864	31	134	434	236	27	2
4	3,265	14	38	485	1,928	781	19
5	2,616	4	10	83	516	1,987	16
6[a]	318	5	5	15	24	5	264
Totals	7,223	118	244	1,048	2,709	2,802	302

[a]A "don't know" response.

ceived an overall satisfaction score of 4. Thus 96 percent of the questionnaires predicted to be a 5 were actually either a 4 or a 5.

From the second perspective, it is seen that the lowest satisfaction score was actually reported on 118 surveys. Thus only 10 percent of the actual lowest scores were correctly predicted by the equation. The highest satisfaction score was actually reported on 2,802 surveys, whereas the equation predicted that 1,987 would receive the highest score.

The multiple regression equation underestimated both the low and the high extremes. The poorest performance was with the most dissatisfied customers. This may indicate that the performance attributes are better suited for predicting satisfied customers than for predicting dissatisfied customers.

Interpreting Multiple Regression Results

Multiple regression analyses are easy to generate with available computing technology. Unfortunately, however, the results of a multiple regression analysis may be very difficult to interpret without the help of a professional statistician.

Notice, for example, that the coefficients of four performance attributes are negative. On the surface, this would imply that overall satisfaction improves when satisfaction with an individual attribute declines. This interpretation is obviously not correct. A professional statistician will recognize this as a problem created by multicollinearity.

Multicollinearity occurs when certain performance attributes are highly correlated with other performance attributes in the equation. For example, an examination of the mathematical values of the correlation coefficients indicates that "Customer requirements drive the company," "Customer service personnel are responsive," and "Questions are answered quickly" are all highly correlated with each other.

When multicollinearity exists, the overall prediction equation may be accurate even though the signs associated with some performance attributes may be reversed. This explanation is clear to a statistician, but it usually will not satisfy a company president.

The existence of multicollinearity also creates problems when the importance of individual performance attributes is analyzed. For example, not all of the performance attributes may be necessary to adequately predict overall satisfaction. The selection of the performance attributes to include in the final equation is determined by statistical significance tests. Multicollinearity will exert an influence on the results of these tests.

Suppose that a performance attribute currently in the equation is highly correlated with another attribute that is a candidate for inclusion. Since the two attributes are highly correlated, little additional predictive information will be gained by adding the second attribute.

The statistical analysis will conclude that the candidate attribute should not be included in the equation. This does not imply that this attribute is not important, but only that the predictive value of the equation is not enhanced given that the other attribute is already in the equation.

Multiple regression results are difficult to interpret if the performance attributes are highly correlated with each other. Other statistical techniques (such as factor analysis and correspondence analysis) exploit these correlations to further explain and interpret the results.

Multiple regression is a valuable statistical tool. Readily available hardware and software contribute to the popularity of the technique. Multiple regression, however, is frequently misused because the underlying assumptions and theory are not understood. Almost every introductory statistics text discusses multiple regression. One of the most respected books devoted exclusively to multiple regression is the Draper and Smith text.

Discriminant Analysis

The performance attributes relating to satisfied customers may not be the same attributes that relate to dissatisfied customers. Discriminant analysis can determine if the set of performance attributes effectively distinguishes between satisfied and dissatisfied customers.

Table 11.3 illustrates how discriminant analysis can help analyze the predictive accuracy of the performance attributes. The table is analogous to Table 11.2, the multiple regression table. Consistent with the multiple regression analysis, the discriminant equation was developed using survey data from the previous quarter.

The discriminant equation predicted that 174 questionnaires would receive the lowest overall satisfaction score. This was a correct prediction in 61 cases. At the other extreme, the equation predicted 3,228 questionnaires would receive the highest possible score. This was correct for 2,270 of the cases. Furthermore, a total of 3,061 of the 3,228 questionnaires received either a 4 or a 5.

On the other hand, only 118 questionnaires actually resulted in the lowest score and only 2,802 questionnaires resulted in the highest score. The discriminant analysis overestimated both extremes.

Statistics from a discriminant analysis can be used to determine what specific performance attributes are most influential in developing the predictions. This can provide valuable insight into determining the attributes most associated with both satis-

Table 11.3

Overall Prediction Accuracy of the Discriminant Equation

Predicted Overall Satisfaction		Actual Overall Satisfaction Rating					
Rating	Number	1	2	3	4	5	6[a]
1	174	61	69	25	13	5	1
2	108	17	39	44	6	2	0
3	537	13	77	293	139	14	1
4	2,871	17	40	545	1,744	508	17
5	3,228	6	15	127	791	2,270	19
6[a]	305	4	4	14	16	3	264
Totals	7,223	118	244	1,048	2,709	2,802	302

[a] A "don't know" response.

fied and dissatisfied customers. The issue of distinguishing among satisfied and dissatisfied customers will be discussed again in the "Correspondence Analysis" section later in this chapter.

Klecka provides a good introduction to discriminant analysis. The Cooley and Lohnes text is a classic reference for a more technical description.

Factor Analysis

Factor analysis is used to study the patterns of correlations existing among the performance attributes. The performance attributes are combined to form a set of factors (often called *dimensions*). The performance attributes are therefore grouped into a smaller set of unifying dimensions.

Factor analysis is used to investigate the nature and number of underlying dimensions in the survey data. The technique has three major applications in customer satisfaction research:

1. Phase 1 research: guidance in selecting an appropriate set of performance attributes.

2. Phase 2 research: guidance in establishing survey validity.

3. Phase 3 research: discovering relationships in survey data that are not evident when using cross-tabulations or other elementary statistical techniques.

A score (called a *factor loading*) is calculated for every survey question on each factor. Questions with high factor loadings on a given factor should form a logical, easy-to-interpret dimension. High scores do not imply outstanding performance; they merely indicate which performance attributes are grouped together to form a dimension.

For example, the first six attributes in the following illustration (factor loadings from 0.90553 to 0.76555) identify a dimension associated with product quality (identifying quality and rectifying unacceptable quality):

Factor Loading	Company	Performance Attribute
0.90553	PVC Resins	Resin is not contaminated.
0.88699	Plastic Polymers	Resin is not contaminated.
0.87761	Industrial Chemical	Resin is not contaminated.
0.79575	PVC Resins	Warranty claims are handled promptly.
0.77461	Plastic Polymers	Warranty claims are handled promptly.
0.76555	Industrial Chemical	Warranty claims are handled promptly.
0.23719	PVC Resins	Price is competitive.
0.17773	Plastic Polymers	Shipments are delivered to specifications.

The two factor loadings immediately following the first six are reported to illustrate how the scores decline sharply from 0.76555 to 0.23719 following the attributes associated with product quality.

The survey questionnaire consisted of 42 questions: an overall rating and individual ratings for 13 performance attributes for each of the three companies. The factor loadings for the first three factors are reported in Table 11.4.

The 14 questions associated with PVC Resins received the highest loadings on the first factor. Notice the sharp decline in factor-loading scores for the first factor following these 14 attributes.

The 14 performance attributes for Industrial Chemical received the highest loadings on the second factor, and the 14 performance attributes pertaining to Plastic Polymers received the highest loadings on the third factor. In each case, a rapid decline in factor-loading scores occurred after the first 14 attributes.

The first three dimensions, therefore, are interpreted as "PVC Resins," "Industrial Chemical," and "Plastic Polymers." These clearly interpretable dimensions indicate that customers can effectively differentiate among the three companies.

A three-dimensional plot of these three factors is presented in Exhibit 11.1 on page 158. The 14 questions concerning PVC Resins are represented by balls. The stars represent the 14 questions concerning Industrial Chemical. The 14 questions concerning Plastic Polymers are represented by flags.

Plots of the three individual companies are separately displayed on pages 159–161 in Exhibits 11.2 (PVC Resins), 11.3 (Industrial Chemical), and 11.4 (Plastic Polymers). The plots provide an indication of how customers perceive similarities and differences among the three companies.

Attributes that are similar tend to be grouped together. Thus the attributes nearest the overall satisfaction rating are the most closely related to overall satisfaction. Distances may be difficult to decipher in three dimensions. To assist in interpreting the plots, the Euclidian distance from each point to the overall satisfaction rating is presented in Table 11.5 on page 162.

The range of distances is greatest for Plastic Polymers. This is the sponsoring company and the company with which customers have the greatest familiarity and experience. Customers can compare and contrast the performance attributes for Plastic Polymers with the most precision. Therefore the distances between the attributes tend to be greater.

Table 11.4

Factor Analysis Loadings

Factor 1	Factor 2	Factor 3	
0.87851	0.23325	0.06238	PVC Resins—The company is professional in business dealings.
0.86685	0.21909	0.12678	PVC Resins—Problems are handled effectively.
0.85575	0.23548	0.05710	PVC Resins—Customer requirements drive the company.
0.84825	0.23456	0.08752	PVC Resins—Questions are answered quickly.
0.83300	0.23555	0.2958	PVC Resins—Just-in-time delivery schedules are met.
0.81437	0.22934	0.01790	PVC Resins—Customer service personnel are responsive.
0.80532	0.22507	0.02152	PVC Resins—Shipments are delivered to specifications.
0.76725	0.23819	0.03594	PVC Resins—Resin is not contaminated.
0.75003	0.21993	0.02623	PVC Resins—Office staff is courteous.
0.72758	0.22600	0.02934	PVC Resins—Billing is accurate.
0.71486	0.21818	0.01554	PVC Resins—Technical support personnel are knowledgeable.
0.71186	0.18571	0.05214	PVC Resins—Overall satisfaction.
0.69431	0.22922	0.04373	PVC Resins—Warranty claims are handled promptly.
0.67224	0.21380	0.00587	PVC Resins—Price is competitive.
0.27175	**0.78315**	0.02787	Industrial Chemical—Customer service personnel are responsive.
0.27118	**0.68673**	0.03170	Industrial Chemical—Billing is accurate.
0.27053	**0.82936**	0.7615	Industrial Chemical—customer requirements drive the company.
0.26910	**0.66202**	0.02336	Industrial Chemical—Warranty claims are handled promptly.

continued

Factor 1	Factor 2	Factor 3	
0.26746	**0.67043**	0.02778	Industrial Chemical—Technical support personnel are knowledgeable.
0.26587	**0.73701**	0.03126	Industrial Chemical—Overall satisfaction.
0.26121	**0.76035**	0.03437	Industrial Chemical—Resin is not contaminated.
0.24469	**0.96400**	0.06527	Industrial Chemical—Company is professional in business dealings.
0.24182	**0.84408**	0.09957	Industrial Chemical—Questions are answered quickly.
0.23877	**0.82912**	0.04381	Industrial Chemical—Just-in-time delivery schedules are met.
0.23727	**0.79961**	0.04412	Industrial Chemical—Shipments are delivered to specifications.
0.23713	**0.85537**	0.13311	Industrial Chemical—Problems are handled effectively.
0.23583	**0.66372**	0.00243	Industrial Chemical—Price is competitive.
0.22392	**0.75738**	0.01619	Industrial Chemical—Office staff is courteous.
0.19667	0.16058	**0.36573**	Plastic Polymers—Warranty claims are handled promptly.
0.18135	0.17006	**0.57224**	Plastic Polymers—Customer requirements drive the company.
0.17763	0.15627	**0.47736**	Plastic Polymers—Customer service personnel are responsive.
0.16949	0.14732	**0.30431**	Plastic Polymers—Billing is accurate.
0.16778	0.15715	**0.41118**	Plastic Polymers—Resin is not contaminated.
0.16721	0.16063	**0.33673**	Plastic Polymers—Technical support personnel are knowledgeable.
0.16679	0.15984	**0.65519**	Plastic Polymers—The company is professional in business dealings.
0.15899	0.15376	**0.33302**	Plastic Polymers—Price is competitive.
0.15648	0.15919	**0.50627**	Plastic Polymers—Just-in-time delivery schedules are met.

Factor 1	Factor 2	Factor 3	
0.15404	0.17487	**0.82963**	Plastic Polymers—Questions are answered quickly.
0.14622	0.13523	**0.36912**	Plastic Polymers—Office staff is courteous.
0.14170	0.14390	**0.90140**	Plastic Polymers—Problems are handled effectively.
0.13676	0.15452	**0.45244**	Plastic Polymers—Shipments are delivered to specifications.
0.10537	0.13378	**0.62807**	Plastic Polymers—Overall satisfaction.

The attributes nearest to overall satisfaction for Plastic Polymers are:

■ The company is professional in business dealings.

■ Questions are answered quickly.

■ Customer requirements drive the company.

■ Problems are handled effectively.

Plastic Polymers excels in the humanistic factors, a conclusion that is consistent with the correlation analysis discussed earlier in this chapter. For this company, technical support, warranty claim handling, competitive pricing, and accurate billing are the most distant from overall satisfaction.

Satisfaction with PVC Resins tends to be highest because of the courteous office staff and the ability to deliver shipments to specification without contamination. On the negative side, the performance attributes furthest from overall satisfaction are quick answers to questions, customer requirements driving the company, problems being handled effectively, and the company being professional in business dealings.

Customer satisfaction with Industrial Chemical arises from shipments delivered to specifications, responsive customer service personnel, a courteous office staff, and meeting just-in-time delivery schedules. The least favorable performance attributes are billing, technical support, and handling of warranty claims.

Exhibit 11.1

Factor Loading Pot

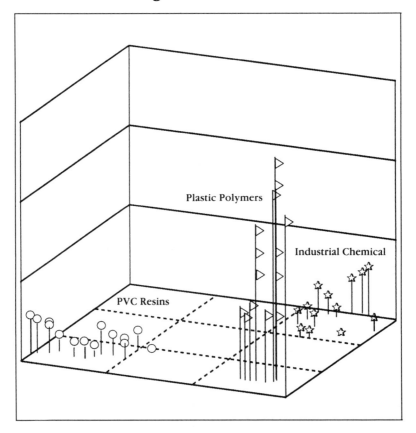

Plastic Polymers

Industrial Chemical

PVC Resins

Factor analysis almost always provides interesting and exciting insights into survey data. Numerous technical decisions, however, are necessary to properly analyze and interpret the results. For example, several variations of input data are possible. The number of statistically significant factors must be determined, and geometrical rotation procedures to help interpret results must be considered.

An in-depth discussion of the practical and technical details of factor analysis would require a separate volume. Rummel presents a good nontechnical introduction to factor analysis. The Cooley and Lohnes text is a prominent reference for technical information.

Exhibit 11.2

PVC Resins: Factor Loadings

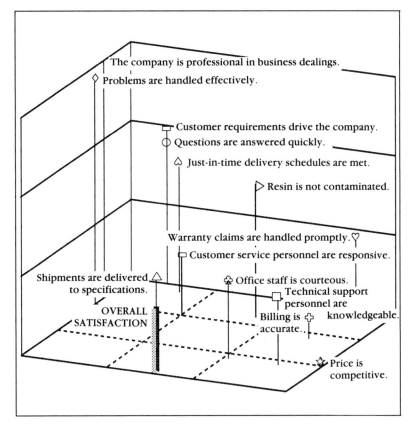

Urban and Hauser provide details on how factor analysis can be used to generate visual interpretations of statistical results.

Correspondence Analysis

Correspondence analysis is a mathematical technique used to develop perceptual maps. Customer satisfaction research is an ideal application for perceptual mapping, since relationships among

Exhibit 11.3

Industrial Chemical: Factor Loadings

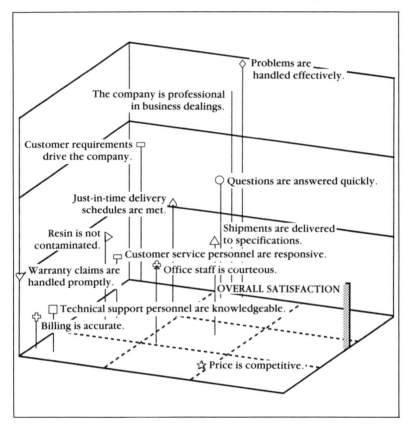

variables such as performance attributes, demographics, and competitors can be investigated.

These relationships are visually portrayed by the relative positions of points on a two- or three-dimensional perceptual map. Points that cluster together reveal performance attributes, demographic characteristics, and companies that are closely related. Points that are further apart are less closely related. The distance between the points, therefore, represents the degree of relationship between the variables.

Correspondence analysis analyzes the joint occurrence of row and column variables. The technique is perfectly suited for data

Exhibit 11.4

Plastic Polymers: Factor Loadings

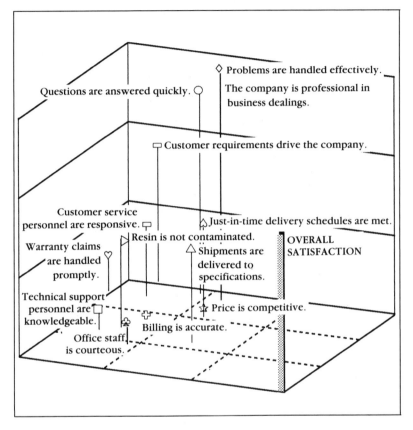

represented as cross-tabulations. For example, columns can depict companies while rows can portray performance attributes. The row and column percentages are reconciled by weighting the categories to best summarize the correlations among them.

Advantages and Disadvantages of Correspondence Analysis

Correspondence analysis offers significant advantages over other statistical techniques. Factor analysis, for example, can analyze row variables (i.e., performance attributes) or column variables

Table 11.5

Distances from Performance Attributes to Overall Satisfaction

PVC Resins

0.0313	Office staff is courteous.
0.0409	Shipments are delivered to specifications.
0.0448	Resin is not contaminated.
0.0613	Customer service personnel are responsive.
0.0642	Billing is accurate.
0.0642	Technical support personnel are knowledgeable.
0.0826	Warranty claims are handled promptly.
0.0917	Just-in-time delivery schedules are met.
0.1022	Price is competitive.
0.1119	Questions are answered quickly.
0.1136	Customer requirements drive the company.
0.1432	Problems are handled effectively.
0.1536	The company is professional in business dealings.

Industrial Chemical

0.0468	Shipments are delivered to specifications.
0.0792	Customer service personnel are responsive.
0.0821	Office staff is courteous.
0.0823	Just-in-time delivery schedules are met.
0.0905	Resin is not contaminated.
0.0986	Questions are answered quickly.
0.1043	Customer requirements drive the company.
0.1267	Price is competitive.
0.1327	The company is professional in business dealings.
0.1399	Problems are handled effectively.
0.1506	Billing is accurate.
0.1551	Technical support personnel are knowledgeable.
0.1620	Warranty claims are handled promptly.

Plastic Polymers

0.0979	Company is professional in business dealings.
0.1013	Questions are answered quickly.
0.1526	Customer requirements drive the company.
0.1528	Problems are handled effectively.
0.1807	Just-in-time delivery schedules are met.
0.1968	Customer service personnel are responsive.
0.2291	Shipments are delivered to specifications.
0.2510	Resin is not contaminated.
0.3120	Office staff is courteous.
0.3518	Technical support personnel are knowledgeable.
0.3559	Warranty claims are handled promptly.
0.3898	Price is competitive.
0.3927	Billing is accurate.

(i.e., companies), but it cannot analyze both simultaneously. Correspondence analysis combines both row and column information in the same analysis.

Another advantage of correspondence analysis is that physical interpretations of the axes are not necessary. Correspondence analysis relies on point-to-point distances rather than distances from axes. In fact, the axes are usually not shown on correspondence analysis maps.

A potential drawback to correspondence analysis is that a significant portion of the individual data is lost, since the technique uses only cross-tabulations. Other mathematical methods employed to implement perceptual maps use the entire set of data, not just the summary tabulations.

Correspondence analysis is a descriptive technique providing qualitative information of an exploratory nature. Multiple regression and discriminate analysis are quantitative techniques where, for example, overall satisfaction can be predicted on the basis of a mathematical equation.

Analyzing Characteristics of Satisfied Customers

Exhibit 11.5 is a perceptual map depicting satisfied customers. The map was developed from cross-tabulations of the number of very favorable responses for each row (performance attribute) and column (company) combination. Each point is represented by an asterisk (*). A description of the point is presented to the right of the asterisk. On some of the maps, the descriptive information is to the left of the asterisk because of space limitations.

The exhibit shows that overall satisfaction and satisfaction with Plastic Polymers are in very close agreement. This is because the perceptual map reflects very satisfied customers and Plastic Polymers is the sponsoring company. A close relationship between overall satisfaction and, for example, Industrial Chemical would be expected if the interviews had been conducted with customers of Industrial Chemical.

The attribute nearest to PVC Resins is "Office staff is courteous." The attributes closest to Industrial Chemical are "Just-in-time deliveries are met" and "Shipments are delivered to specifications." Two other attributes, "Office staff is courteous" and "Customer service personnel are responsive" are also near Indus-

Exhibit 11.5

Very Satisfied Customers: Perceptual Map

*Resin is not contaminated.

*Billing is accurate.

*PVC RESIN

*Office staff is courteous.

*INDUSTRIAL CHEMICAL
*Just-in-time deliveries are met.
    *Shipments are delivered to specifications.

*Customer service personnel are responsive.

*Customer requirements drive the company.

    *The company is professional in business
dealings.

*Warranty claims are handled promptly.

*Technical support personnel are knowledgeable.
        *Problems are handled effectively.
*PLASTIC POLYMERS
*OVERALL SATISFACTION

            *Price is competitive.

*Questions are answered quickly.

trial Chemical. These results are in agreement with the factor analysis conclusions presented in the preceding section.

The attributes contributing to satisfaction with Plastic Polymers are "Problems are handled effectively," "Technical support personnel are knowledgeable," "Price is competitive," and "Questions are answered quickly."

Analyzing Characteristics of Dissatisfied Customers

Exhibit 11.6 is a similar perceptual map depicting very dissatisfied customers. Handling of warranty claims is the problem attribute most closely associated with dissatisfied customers. Accurate billing, on the other hand, appears to be least closely associated with poor overall satisfaction ratings.

Customers dissatisfied with PVC Resins tend to focus on humanistic attributes: "Customer requirements drive the company," "Customer service personnel are responsive," and "The company is professional in business dealings."

Industrial Chemical has problems with physical deliveries, as evidenced by customer concern with just-in-time delivery schedules, contaminated resin, and shipments delivered to specifications. Plastic Polymers must improve in answering questions quickly and stressing office staff courtesy.

Comparing Correspondence Analysis and Factor Analysis Results

A few differences can be detected between the correspondence analysis and factor analysis results. These differences occur because the correspondence analysis used only very satisfied (or very dissatisfied) responses, whereas the factor analysis used the entire set of responses. Correspondence analysis also uses cross-tabulations, which aggregate the data, whereas factor analysis uses each individual survey response without any aggregation.

Correspondence analysis produces perceptual maps that are easy to understand and interpret. The underlying mathematics, however, is complex: The distances among attributes and companies are derived using sophisticated statistical techniques.

Correspondence analysis is an exciting technique for analyzing and interpreting survey data. Weller and Romney provide an

Exhibit 11.6

Very Dissatisfied Customers:
Perceptual Map

*Billing is accurate.

*The company is professional in business dealings.
*Customer requirements drive the company.

*PVC RESIN

Customer service personnel are responsive.*

*Warranty claims are handled promptly.
*OVERALL
SATISFACTION

*Technical support personnel are knowledgeable.
*Problems are handled effectively.
Office staff is courteous*.
Shipments are delivered to specifications.*   *Questions
are answered quickly.
*Resin is not contaminated.
*INDUSTRIAL CHEMICAL   *PLASTIC POLYMERS
*Just-in-time deliveries are met.

*Price is competitive.

excellent introduction to correspondence analysis. The Hoffman and Franke text is another good reference.

Conclusions from the Statistical Analysis

The correlation coefficients (Table 11.1) and the factor analysis results (Table 11.5) indicate the performance attributes that Plastic Polymers customers associate most closely with overall satisfaction. These attributes are quick answers to questions, effective handling of problems, professional business dealings, customer requirements driving a company, and meeting just-in-time delivery schedules.

The survey results, unfortunately, indicate that these attributes did not receive the highest average scores. The averages reveal that customers view the office staff as courteous, technical support as knowledgeable, and customer service personnel as responsive. Nevertheless, the critical issues of handling problems effectively and answering questions quickly receive lower average scores.

A clue to understanding this contradiction is the lower average scores associated with meeting just-in-time delivery schedules and handling warranty claims. Although its personnel are courteous and knowledgeable, the company is not satisfying the customers' delivery and warranty expectations.

The perceptual map for very satisfied customers (Exhibit 11.5) indicates that effective handling of problems, knowledgeable technical-support personnel, and answering questions quickly are highly related to overall satisfaction. Very satisfied customers also view Plastic Polymers' price as competitive.

The perceptual map for very dissatisfied customers (Exhibit 11.6) indicates that answering questions quickly, handling problems effectively, and having a courteous office staff are negatives for Plastic Polymers. Directly measurable causes of dissatisfaction are shipments not being delivered to specifications and not meeting just-in-time delivery schedules.

A combination of discussions with Plastic Polymers personnel and in-depth interviews with dissatisfied customers uncovered two serious problems:

1. Plastic Polymers' shipment-tracking system was not technically capable of producing quick answers to questions about just-in-time delivery status. This frustrated customers when dealing with Plastic Polymers' office and customer service personnel.

2. The company's customer service and technical support departments were highly trained to help customers select the correct resin for the application specifications. Neither department, however, was geared to respond quickly to problems created by shipments not delivered to the required specifications.

Plastic Polymers initiated quality teams to develop and implement solutions to these two problems. Their successful resolution resulted in a reduction in the number of dissatisfied customers. Increased market share occurred, largely at the expense of Industrial Chemical sales.

Satisfied customers viewed Industrial Chemical's ability to meet just-in-time schedules and to deliver to specifications as company strengths. Very dissatisfied customers, however, viewed the same two performance attributes as severe company weaknesses. Although Industrial Chemical has a superior reputation in these areas, that reputation works against the company when performance failures occur. Knowledgeable sales reps of Plastic Polymers capitalize on these occasional failures in order to obtain business from Industrial Chemical customers.

Conjoint Analysis

Customer satisfaction survey data generate a wealth of information that can be used to establish priorities and develop strategies for improvement. Some examples were given in the preceding section, and others will be presented in Chapter 13. Mathematical modeling procedures can help predict the consequences of using different improvement strategies. Conjoint analysis is one of the modeling techniques most used in conjunction with customer satisfaction research.

Conjoint analysis is used to evaluate the impacts of various trade-offs that consumers make when buying products and services. This is a logical extension of customer satisfaction research, since important trade-off decisions usually involve the critical performance attributes identified by the satisfaction research.

A conjoint analysis involves implementation of five major steps:

1. Identifying trade-off choices among the critical performance attributes

2. Developing an experimental design to measure trade-offs

3. Conducting consumer surveys to implement the experimental design

4. Computing utility functions that measure the importance of the various trade-offs

5. Analyzing the impact of changes in the product or service

A variety of highly technical methodologies has been developed to implement conjoint analysis. Although this is a very specialized subject, the general concepts can be illustrated with a continuation of the polyvinyl chloride resin case study of the preceding sections of this chapter.

Plastic Polymers conducted a conjoint analysis to better understand the purchasing motivations of smaller-volume customers. Three critical performance attributes were specifically selected for this study: price, delivery schedules, and technical support.

A separate questionnaire, independent of the customer satisfaction survey, had to be developed. Conjoint analysis is implemented by asking customers to evaluate different combinations of product characteristics. In this case study, customers evaluated 12 different combinations by rating the likelihood of purchasing the product defined by each of the 12 scenarios. Customers used a 5-point rating scale ranging from "very likely to purchase" to "very unlikely to purchase."

The 12 scenarios involved 3 different prices ($.79, $.80, and $.81 per pound), a choice between just-in-time delivery and delivery within plus or minus one day of schedule, and the presence or absence of technical support.

Price differentials of $.01 per pound are significant since larger customers purchase millions of pounds of the product annually. Because of the very competitive marketplace, $.01-per-pound differences are very important, even to smaller-volume customers.

Just-in-time delivery was selected because Plastic Polymers needed to develop better information about the importance of delivery schedules to its smaller customers. The presence or absence of technical support was selected for the same reason.

The levels of the three performance attributes can be combined in the following 12 arrangements:

Scenario	Price	Technical Support	Delivery Time
1	$.81	Yes	± 1 day
2	.79	Yes	± 1 day
3	.81	No	Just-in-time
4	.80	No	± 1 day
5	.80	No	Just-in-time
6	.81	No	± 1 day
7	.80	Yes	Just-in-time
8	.80	Yes	± 1 day
9	.79	No	± 1 day
10	.79	No	Just-in-time
11	.79	Yes	Just-in-time
12	.81	Yes	Just-in-time

In this application, customers rated all 12 scenarios. Some studies are designed so that not all of the combinations are evaluated. In more sophisticated applications, decisions are made about the combinations to be evaluated while the interview is progressing. For example, if a customer's pattern of responses indicated that technical support was not necessary or desired, future combinations involving changes in technical support levels would be eliminated.

Scenario 11 is clearly the best choice of the 12, since it offers the lowest price combined with both technical support and just-in-time delivery. Scenario 10, however, is equally attractive if technical support is not desired. Scenario 2 is also attractive if just-in-time delivery is not important and delivery within one day is acceptable. Scenario 6 is very unattractive since the highest price is combined with neither technical support nor just-in-time delivery.

A survey of 100 smaller-volume customers was conducted. The results were analyzed by a conjoint analysis software package that computed the following market shares for each of the 12 scenarios:

Scenario	Market Share Percentage
1	1%
2	20
3	0
4	0
5	0
6	0
7	2
8	1
9	1
10	2
11	61
12	2

The importance of technical support among the smaller-volume customers is clearly evidenced by the poor market share associated with Scenario 10. Just-in-time delivery is not as important, since Scenario 2 generated a reasonable market share.

Market share changes based on various new combinations of the three attributes can be estimated. Suppose, for example, that the price in Scenario 11 is raised by $.005 per pound. The new market share estimates indicate that Scenario 11 drops from 61 percent to 47 percent, while Scenario 2 increases from 20 percent to 42 percent. A significant number of customers will shift to

Scenario 2, sacrificing just-in-time delivery for a price reduction of $.005 per pound. Numerous scenarios of this nature can be tested to investigate the sensitivity of market share to changes in the performance attributes.

Surveys involving comparisons of product alternatives are difficult to conduct using telephone interviews. Consumer studies are often implemented using shopping-mall interviews, whereas business-to-business surveys sometimes use computer disks. In the latter surveys, a customer is interviewed by telephone and then asked to complete the conjoint survey from a disk that is received in the mail. Mail questionnaires filled out on paper is another alternative for both consumer and business-to-business studies.

12

Integrating Company Information in the Research Process

*T*elephone and mail surveys are the cornerstones of customer satisfaction research. Every organization, however, has a wealth of additional customer satisfaction knowledge that is not based directly on survey results. This indirect information includes sales volume, market share, number of complaints, dollar amount of warranty payments, and similar data.

Complaint analysis, for example, should include at least the following information:

1. Counts of complaints by representative categories:
   a. product quality
   b. service quality
   c. out-of-stock products
   d. products not delivered on time
   e. products damaged during shipping
   f. errors in billing

2. Documentation of all complaints received

3. Documentation of who receives and acts on the complaints

4. Standards for responding to complaints

Such analysis, of course, represents information only about formal complaints, and does not include the influential criticisms offered to friends and relatives.

Satisfaction, Complaints, and Repurchase Intentions

The relationships among satisfaction, complaints, and repurchase intentions appear to be rather complex. One might guess that dissatisfaction generates complaints and negative repurchase intentions and that satisfaction generates positive repurchase intentions. Researchers have reported, however, that the three variables occur in virtually every combination.

Because not all dissatisfied customers register complaints, the absence of a complaint does not necessarily indicate satisfaction. Jacoby and Jaccard provide evidence that satisfied customers also complain; thus the presence of a complaint does not necessarily indicate dissatisfaction.

Many researchers have found that repurchase intentions are increased if complaints are handled quickly and in a positive manner. Gilly's text is a good reference on this subject. Some researchers believe that complaints tend to enhance repurchase decisions even if the complaints are not handled in a satisfactory manner. Other researchers provide evidence to the contrary. Studies by TARP and by Halstead and Page discuss these contrasting views.

The relationships among satisfaction, complaints, and repurchase intentions are influenced by the type and cost of the product or service, by the expense or difficulty of complaining, and by demographic and psychographic characteristics of the purchasers. Since the relationships are complicated, customer satisfaction research should contrast the satisfaction and repurchase-intention scores of complainers and noncomplainers. This can be accomplished by denoting in advance which customers in the survey registered complaints in the past.

Indirect Measurements Are Passive

Indirect measurements such as complaints are very important and must be effectively monitored and correlated with formal survey results. They are not dynamic indicators of customer satisfaction, however, because they are indirect and passive.

The measurements are passive because they are not directly initiated by the company to determine customer satisfaction. They do not measure the intensity or direction of satisfaction. The focus, for example, should not be on the number of complaints but on eliminating the behaviors and situations that create complaints.

Indirect measures are also somewhat lethargic indicators of satisfaction or dissatisfaction. Customer satisfaction will decline before sales decreases are observed. Satisfaction research, therefore, is a more effective early warning indicator than either sales or market share trends. Conversely, increases in satisfaction provide positive indicators that are essential in tactical and strategic planning.

Indirect Measurements Should Be Related to Customer Satisfaction

Customer satisfaction survey results must be coordinated and correlated with these other sources of satisfaction information. Trends in customer satisfaction survey data, for example, should be consistent with changes and patterns in customer complaints (although a lag may exist). Informal conversations with customers should reflect the same type of information that is generated in the formal survey. These reality checks help ensure that goals, objectives, strategies, and plans are developed using the maximum amount of consistent and reliable information.

The indirect measurements are critically important when customer lists are impossible or impractical to obtain. Fast-food restaurants, grocery stores, gas stations, and music stores in shopping malls do not always know who shops at their establishments.

The Malcolm Baldrige award requirements, examined in the next section, emphasize the importance of coordinating indirect measures of customer satisfaction. The chapter concludes with a detailed example of how Burger King uses different methodologies to develop a composite measure of customer satisfaction.

Multiple Sources of Customer Satisfaction Information

The Malcolm Baldrige Award requirements emphasize the coordination and integration of multiple sources of customer satisfaction information. Specific examples taken from the current requirements are:

■ Cross-comparisons with other key data and information such as complaints, losses and gains of customers, and performance data that may yield information on customer requirements and expectations and on key product and service features

■ Correlation of satisfaction results with other satisfaction indicators such as complaints and gains and losses of customers

■ Trends in major adverse indicators such as complaints, claims, refunds, mandatory recalls, returns, repeat services, replacements, downgrades, repairs, warranty costs, and warranty work

Here are two examples of information used to develop a coordinated and integrated view of customer satisfaction. CalComp (a Lockheed company) relies on the following information:

- Annual survey by outside agency
- A specifically designed survey of service contract customers
- Questionnaires to dealers and distributors
- Field sales survey input
- Customer service input
- Technical product support data
- Telemarketing data
- Trade journal benchmarking
- Contacting customers

SuperAmerica (a subsidiary of Ashland Oil) combines the following data to develop customer satisfaction intelligence:

- Inventory turn reports
- SAMI reports
- Velocity reports (movement of products)
- On-site market research
- Off-site focus groups (customer and noncustomer)
- Telephone surveys
- Customer mailers
- Mystery shoppers
- Competition surveys
- Industry-related publications

A comprehensive example of how Burger King develops a customer satisfaction index is presented in the following section.

Burger King: An In-Depth Example

Burger King Corporation provides an excellent example of how different sources of information are effectively combined in customer satisfaction research. Note especially how Burger King addresses these important issues:

1. Use of different research methodologies to provide an overall assessment of customer satisfaction

2. Use of creative methods when names and addresses of customers are not readily available

3. How satisfaction is considered both globally and locally

4. How customer satisfaction is incorporated in the company culture

5. How research results are communicated within the organization

6. How satisfied customers influence bottom-line profits

The following description of Burger King's customer satisfaction research was developed by Natalie Blacher, Director of Competitive and Industry Research at Burger King.

> The fast-food industry is clearly being challenged by a very intense competitive and economic environment. Most companies have engaged in heavy promotional activity and introduced a multitude of new products in order to reignite customers' interest in patronizing fast-food restaurants. Although these initiatives are certainly necessary, they tend to be short-term remedies rather than ones that fundamentally change purchasing behavior.

> Burger King firmly believes that a sustainable competitive advantage will be realized through superior customer service. A merely acceptable customer experience no longer suffices. Today's customer has far too many choices, and expectations about dining experiences have heightened considerably.

> Burger King Corporation has always been dedicated to enhancing quality and customer satisfaction. Over the past decade, we have routinely measured customer satisfaction at Burger King and our competitors. This research was very traditional in nature and provided us with the critical elements of customer satisfaction and dissatisfaction for our restaurant system in general.

Yet, there was a fundamental shortcoming with this research. A national problem may not be directly applicable to an individual restaurant which is plagued by specific deficiencies. To illustrate, order accuracy is a major concern on a national basis. However, a particular restaurant may be delivering the right order but not with the appropriate speed.

Therefore, Burger King's objective was to implement a Brand Delivery program that measures how successfully we meet both our internally prescribed operational standards and the needs and expectations of our customers at each and every restaurant. We wanted to ensure that the information was relevant and actionable.

There are three sources of "feedback" which form a composite measure known as the Brand Delivery Index (BDI). The three sources of feedback are a toll-free consumer relations 1-800 phone line, monthly mystery shops, and a technical internal audit program called the Quality Assurance Audit.

Customer Response 1-800 Hotline: Burger King operates a 24-hour toll-free number daily in the United States and Canada for customers to call in with questions, issues, complaints, or praises concerning any aspect of their dining experience. This service is actively promoted in Burger King restaurants on its carry-out bags, trayliners, and posters displayed in the restaurants.

The customer response center receives over 4,000 phone calls per day. Our research indicates that a disgruntled customer can have a powerful and multiplicative effect on future business. A quick and satisfying resolution to a problem can play a major role in building brand loyalty. Over the past year about one-fourth of the customer calls represented some type of complaint, one-third provided positive feedback or praise, and the remaining forty percent of the calls were comments, suggestions, or questions.

The Consumer Response database is a rich source of information about product quality, marketing programs, employee conduct and restaurant operations. Each of the calls is recorded and reported to field management and franchisees on a weekly basis. Summary reports of the calls are generated for specific departments to proactively address issues raised by our customers and respond to other information as appropriate.

It should be noted that only actionable operational complaints are included in the Brand Delivery Index. Any situation which might be considered beyond the control of an individual restaurant, such as national advertising campaigns, policies and procedures, are excluded from the Brand Delivery Index calculation.

Mystery Shopper Program: The mystery shop program is the second component of the BDI. Mystery shoppers are commissioned by Burger King Corporation to anonymously visit restaurants and evaluate them on speed of service, courtesy, order accuracy, food quality, and the cleanliness and condition of our restaurants.

Mystery shops are conducted once each month for every Burger King restaurant in the system. Mystery shops are rotated between drive-thru and inside visits as well as meal occasion (breakfast, lunch, or dinner).

The questionnaire is oriented towards customer perceptions and not internal operational standards. For example, product temperature is evaluated based upon the shopper's perception rather than using a thermometer and checking it against a fixed operational standard. The scored mystery shop questionnaire is mailed to the restaurant manager and franchisee within two days after the mystery shop is conducted.

Quality Assurance Audit: An internal team of Burger King employees conducts comprehensive operational audits of each restaurant several times annually. These audits are technical in nature and more objective than the mystery shops and consumer response system. The primary focus of these audits is on "behind the counter" activities.

A regression analysis was conducted between the BDI components and sales growth over time. We observed that, in the aggregate, the BDI is a strong predictor of sales performance. Each component was assigned a specific weighting based on the strength of its correlation to sales. In order to create a familiar frame of reference, the index was placed on a 100-point scale.

Both the mystery shop and quality assurance audit were easily converted to 100 points, but we had to develop a straightforward formula for the 1-800 calls. Each complaint is assigned a point value and subtracted from a base of 100. The point value for each complaint varies, depending upon the sales volume of the individual restaurant (lighter-volume restaurants tend to have more complaints, so variable points ensured equitable scoring).

Burger King's Brand Delivery program has served as a catalyst for change at Burger King. First and foremost, the concept of "customer satisfaction" has become deeply embedded within our culture. It is no longer some esoteric notion; it is tangible and real.

From Burger King's 1-800 system and mystery shoppers, we have a much keener sense of what constitutes a truly special experience at our restaurants—in the consumers' own words. The Brand Delivery program has afforded us the opportunity to "model" operational excellence. Similarly, we know those situations and encounters which anger our customers and affect future visitation.

Secondly, Burger King employees at all organizational levels are exceptionally well informed about whether or not we are satisfying the consumer. They can access BDI performance on a monthly basis. Restaurant and operations managers are provided with detailed data on which critical elements of the restaurant experience were deficient.

For the first time in the company's history, Burger King is able to produce a detailed report card for every restaurant in the Burger King system. The BDI takes the guesswork out of determining "what's wrong with this picture." Incentive programs and contests have been effectively linked to BDI improvement.

Thirdly, we can now answer the question: "Does superior customer satisfaction pay off?" It is a resounding YES! Those restaurants with superior BDI scores have significantly higher sales volumes and growth rates.

Over time, the sales gap between high and low BDI restaurants has widened, which suggests that the benefits ascribed to superior customer satisfaction may become more pronounced in the long term. Additionally, in an analysis of Burger King's company-owned restaurants, we found that our top operators were not only achieving better sales but significantly higher profits, as well.

At Burger King, we vigorously believe in the power of superior customer satisfaction. By no means do we feel that we've accomplished our goal of providing a wonderful dining experience each and every day. However, with the Brand Delivery program we have a clear picture of how to get there and how far we have to go.

Indirect Measures Compliment Customer Satisfaction Research

The Burger King example illustrates the importance and usefulness of indirect measures of customer satisfaction. Declining sales may suggest a deterioration in customer satisfaction. The sales figures, however, do not suggest the reasons for the decline in satisfaction. Sales may also be declining for reasons unrelated to customer satisfaction.

Indirect measurements should demonstrate a correlation with the customer satisfaction survey results. Increases in satisfaction, for example, should result in reduced levels of complaints. Indirect measures and survey results compliment each other. Analyses of both sources of information provide a more complete picture of customers' perceptions of a company.

13

Applying the Results

How to Improve Satisfaction

C ustomer satisfaction research creates a wealth of strategic information about customers, the sponsoring company, and competitors. Research filed in a desk drawer, however, will make no impact.

The importance of action is emphasized by CalComp Inc. in describing one objective of its customer satisfaction research: "Gaining market share by taking *specific actions* indicated by customer satisfaction measures." R. L. Manis, Director of Quality at CalComp says, "Customer satisfaction has become the driver of the entire organization in business-planning goals. Our version of total quality management is targeted at customer satisfaction."

Customer satisfaction research results should be highly visible throughout the organization. Although aspects of the research may be considered confidential, employees must be provided feedback so that customer satisfaction becomes institutionalized. Employees must know what the company is trying to accomplish and why it is important. Every employee should know the critical performance attributes. The Malcolm Baldrige award requirements address the importance of employee awareness by requiring:

- A process for ensuring that customer service requirements are understood and responded to throughout the company

- Deployment of requirements and/or standards information to all company units to ensure effective support for customer-contact employees who are expected to meet the company's customer service standards

Implementation strategies must be consistent with the research results. Increased advertising, for example, may not be a rational action for increasing market share if the survey results indicate that customers perceive the product as poor.

Customer expectations must be translated into quantifiable service standards. Actions must be taken to ensure that the service standards are met. Service standards that do not conform to customer expectations will not create satisfaction.

Gaps between Company Perspectives and Customer Expectations

Customer satisfaction research provides an opportunity to compare differences in perceptions among customers, company executives, and other company employees. These differences may identify two critical communication gaps:

- Gaps between the company's perception of customer requirements and the customer's actual expectations

- Gaps between the perceptions of senior management and

the perceptions of the employees in direct contact with customers

These gaps must be eliminated. Senior management objectives determine company goals, and the actions of management impact the company culture. Customer expectations and requirements, however, must be the driving force in developing objectives and influencing company culture. Company perspectives must be synchronized with customer requirements.

A firm should not wait for the customer satisfaction survey results before beginning to contrast company and customer perspectives. The critical performance attributes generated by company executives should be compared with the customers' perspective. Significant differences will highlight critical communication gaps.

Senior management's commitment to customer satisfaction must be communicated to every employee. The expectation that each employee will contribute to improving customer satisfaction should be clearly understood by every employee. Training, communication of expectations, and feedback on accomplishments are critical in closing the gap between the perceptions of senior management and those of other employees.

Analysis of Competitors

Each performance attribute should be analyzed with respect to the sponsoring company and its competitors. Action plans should be generated and implemented based on the answers to these questions:

■ Who are the best-performing companies with respect to each performance attribute? Why are they better than other companies?

■ What performance attributes represent the strongest points for the sponsoring company? How can these strengths be exploited?

- Where is the sponsoring company weakest? How can these weaknesses be rectified?

- Where is each competitor weakest? How can the vulnerability of the competition be exploited?

- What differences exist by demographic or psychographic groups?

- What are the emerging trends for each company?

The answers to these questions determine the plans and priorities that must be established to increase customer satisfaction.

One client, for example, observed substantial geographic differences in survey results after a price increase was announced. The ratings for two performance attributes ("willingness to negotiate prices" and "knowledgeable sales reps") declined dramatically in one region, dropped slightly in another region, but remained stable in a third region.

Further investigation uncovered that each of the three regions used a different method to implement the price increase. Executives in the region where satisfaction scores remained stable conducted personal interviews with major accounts to explain the necessity of the price increase. Detailed letters of explanation prior to the price increase were mailed in the region with a small drop in satisfaction ratings.

The region with the large decline in ratings did not undertake any proactive measures but merely let sales reps attempt to justify the price increase if questions arose after a general announcement occurred in the media. The customer satisfaction survey results provided obvious guidance for implementing future price increases.

Establishing Priorities

The collection of customer satisfaction data is a diagnostic tool that must be translated into two general objectives:

Improve performance relative to the company's past accomplishments

- Improve performance relative to the performance of competititors

The distinction between overall image and specific transactions is important. For example, consider the comments about sales representatives presented in Exhibit 9.1. What themes emerge that are critical from an overall perspective? What themes, although important, are related to a specific situation? Comments concerning overall image suggest the need for company-wide attention, whereas many transaction-related comments can be addressed at local levels.

The organization must consider what areas can be changed: policies and procedures, organizational structure, advertising, communication with customers, price, product availabilty, product service and quality, training, and so on. Executive incentive compensation, for example, should be correlated with customer satisfaction trends. Improving customer satisfaction must be placed on the same level of importance as sales and production goals.

Customer satisfaction is not just the concern of top executives. Every employee must be involved with the process. Performance objectives and performance appraisals should emphasize customer satisfaction. Customer satisfaction goals should be incorporated in sales commission calculations.

Procedures that influence performance appraisals and compensation should be developed after the reliability of the survey has been established. Survey results based on three or four quarters will provide the necessary averages and standard deviations to develop realistic performance standards.

The following case study exemplifies the use of research data to establish priorities in improving customer satisfaction.

CASE STUDY

Establishing Priorities Based on Customer Satisfaction Research

The Physicians' Diagnostic Lab performs diagnostic tests for physicians. The company has implemented advanced technology and innovative procedures to better service the physician groups. Physicians' Diagnostic Lab conducted a telephone survey to determine how the company was perceived in comparison with three major competing

---
Exhibit 13.1

Perceptual Map: What the Office Staff of Physician Groups Consider Important in Choosing a Laboratory

*HOSPITAL LABS INC.

*Convenient location
MIDWEST CLINIC
UNITED MEDICAL RESOURCES

*Speed in getting results
*Ability to schedule patients quickly

*Overall quality of laboratory services
*Lack of quality at
competing facilities

PHYSICIANS' DIAGNOSTIC LAB
    *Unique procedures not available elsewhere

*Reputation of laboratory personnel

laboratories (Hospital Labs Inc., Midwest Clinic, and United Medical Resources). Opinions from both medical staffs and office staffs were obtained, since either could refer work to the four laboratories.

Perceptual maps were developed to analyze the attributes that medical staffs and office staffs thought were most important in choosing a laboratory. As expected, the perceptual map for office staffs (Exhibit 13.1) indicated that the Physicians' Diagnostic Lab was viewed as offering unique procedures not available at the other laboratories.

The medical staffs, however, viewed the four laboratories as interchangeable with no individual distinguishing characteristics (Exhibit 13.2). The choice of laboratory was dependent on location and turnaround speed.

The customer satisfaction research indicates that the Physicians' Diagnostic Lab has not adequately conveyed to the medical staffs the unique capabilities it can offer. Enhancing the image of the laboratory among medical staffs became a major priority for the Physicians' Diagnostic Lab. A series of focus groups with office staff personnel was conducted to better understand the differences in perception between the office and medical staffs.

The qualitative research indicated that the office staff took more time to evaluate the competing laboratories and had more current knowledge of the recent advancements implemented by the Physicians' Diagnostic Lab. The laboratory developed a comprehensive awareness program, including open houses, demonstrations and presentations to change the awareness level among the medical staffs.

The open-ended responses in the original survey suggested another critical priority. Competition existed not only from traditional testing facilities but also from a rapidly growing number of outpatient satellite facilities. These facilities, primarily developed for outpatient surgery and specialty clinic functions, also offered laboratory-testing services. Attitudes and perceptions concerning outpatient facilities were included in later customer satisfaction research surveys.

Developing Strategies

The development of strategy for the improvement of customer satisfaction is illustrated by the following two case studies. Each case study utilizes easily interpreted perceptual maps developed from research data, although similar conclusions can be obtained by using other statistical techniques or by carefully examining cross-tabulations.

Exhibit 13.2

Perceptual Map: What the Medical Staff of Physician Groups Consider Important in Choosing a Laboratory

*Unique procedures not
available elsewhere

*Speed in getting results

*Convenient location
*HOSPITAL LABS INC. *PHYSICIANS' DIAGNOSTIC LAB
*MIDWEST CLINIC   *UNITED MEDICAL RESOURCES
*Ability to schedule patients quickly

Lack of quality at competing facilities*

*Reputation of laboratory personnel

*Overall quality of
laboratory services

C A S E   S T U D Y

Developing Strategies for Improving Customer Satisfaction with a Retail Strip Mall

The management of a suburban retail strip mall, Plaza Place, wished to determine shoppers' perceptions about possible additional stores as part of a proposed expansion of the mall.

A telephone questionnaire was designed using input from on-site interviews with shoppers, personal interviews with community leaders, and a series of focus groups composed of local shoppers. Perceptual maps were used to relate annual household income to responses to three open-ended questions:

What do you like most about shopping in Plaza Place? (Exhibit 13.3)

What do you dislike most about shopping in Plaza Place? (Exhibit 13.4)

What stores would you like added to Plaza Place? (Exhibit 13.5)

The following conclusions, based on annual household income, were developed using the perceptual maps:

The most affluent shoppers (with annual incomes exceeding $100,000) will be attracted to a retail area featuring additional clothing stores with ample selection and variety in an uncrowded shopping atmosphere.

Shoppers with incomes of $50,000 to $100,000 enjoy the convenience of the shopping area but are very price-sensitive. The addition of a restaurant and shoe store will be most appealing to this group.

Shoppers in the $28,000–$50,000 income range will be attracted by the convenience of grocery and department stores featuring competitive prices and abundant parking.

Shoppers with incomes of less than $28,000 are unusual in this suburb. Because of the small number of respondents, distinguishing characteristics for this group are not apparent on the perceptual maps.

continued

Exhibit 13.3

Perceptual Map: What People Like about Shopping in Plaza Place, Classified by Income

```
        *Variety        *Friendly store personnel
                      *Plentiful parking




                    *INCOME: $28,000–$50,000
                    *INCOME: $50,000–$100,000
                          *Close to home
                                    *Location
                               *Convenience




  *INCOME $28,000




                             *INCOME $100,000

                          *Not crowded
```

Similar perceptual maps, categorized by sex and age, were also analyzed. Older shoppers, for example, disliked parking problems and the lack of grocery store competition. The 40- to 50-year-old group found lack of variety in the shopping mall to be a serious disadvantage. This age group will strongly support a restaurant in the mall. The 30- to 39-year-old group will be interested in clothing and grocery stores.

Information from the perceptual maps was combined with three additional types of quantitative data:

1. Satisfaction ratings for specific performance attributes (price, selection, availability, physical appearance of stores, parking, and several other attributes)

Exhibit 13.4

Perceptual Map: What People Dislike about Shopping in Plaza Place, Classified by Income

---

*Shopping area crowded

*INCOME $28,000

*Grocery store is overpriced/needs competition

*INCOME: $50,000–$100,000
                    *Prices

Parking*
*INCOME: $28,000–$50,000
      *Traffic

                    *Lack of selection
                      *Lack of variety
                    *INCOME $100,000

---

2. Estimates of sales leakage by type of purchase (also obtained from the telephone interviews)

3. Demographic analyses of the suburb, surrounding suburbs, and other communities with similar characteristics

This information was used to develop a strategy to attract a targeted demographic group by adding specific types of retail stores to the shopping mall. The projected annual sales (based on the sales leakage estimates) were consistent with sales volumes in similar communities and with estimates generated from both the telephone and on-site interviews.

continued

Exhibit 13.5

Perceptual Map: Stores People Want Added to Plaza Place, Classified by Income

*Department store
*INCOME $28,000–$50,000
*Grocery store

*Women's clothing
    *Men's clothing
    INCOME $100,000
*Children's clothing

INCOME $50,000–$100,000
*Restaurant   *Shoe store

INCOME $28,000

C A S E   S T U D Y

Developing Strategies to Improve the Corporate Image of and Customer Satisfaction with a Local Bank

Security Bank, a well-established and financially conservative bank, had recently opened a branch in a geographic locale well beyond its traditional region. The bank wished to gather customer satisfaction data as a basis for developing strategies to improve its image in the community.

In the survey that was prepared to collect information on Security Bank and on four of its competitors, respondents were asked which of the five banks was best in each of seven key performance measurements: overall satisfaction, best for saving, best for borrowing, most courteous employees, best overall service, best management, and most active in community involvement.

Exhibit 13.6 depicts the relationship between overall satisfaction and various demographic groups. First American Trust is the area's oldest and most established bank. The bank is viewed most favorably by city residents and lower-income and older adults. Second Federal's demographic strength is among males and middle-income respondents. National Bank is strongest among white and younger respondents. Females and middle-income respondents tend to favor Security Bank, while Metro Bank's greatest support is among suburban and upper-income respondents.

Although viewed favorably by female and middle-aged respondents, Security Bank had not yet established unique strengths in its new geographic market. The lack of unique strengths is evident in Exhibit 13.7. Notice that none of the performance attributes is close to Security Bank on the perceptual map. A major objective of the bank was to develop recognizable strengths among the performance attributes.

The favorable perception among females and middle-income respondents helped in the development of initial strategies. Previous research had indicated that females tended to relate most favorably to banks with employees who were concerned and caring and to banks with a strong record of safety and reliability. Middle-aged respondents also tended to favor banks with caring employees and banks actively involved in the community.

Although Security Bank was new to the area, it had an outstanding record of financial responsibility. As a result of the customer satisfaction research, this record was emphasized in the company's advertising and other promotional literature. The company also became more active in community affairs, including the sponsorship of local cultural events. Later surveys indicated that Security Bank was becoming more visible among middle-aged respondents. Community involvement and best-management ratings showed a movement toward Security Bank. After the initial success, the bank developed strategies for other demographic groups and substantially increased its total market share.

continued

Exhibit 13.6

Demographic Perceptual Map: The Bank That Most Satisfies Customer Expectations

*Nonwhite

       *City resident   *Lower-income

          *FIRST AMERICAN TRUST

              *Older adult

          *SECOND FEDERAL

*Male   *Middle-aged

              *White
*NATIONAL BANK

*Younger adult

    *Female

*SECURITY BANK

     *Middle-aged adult

               *Suburban resident

       *Upper-income   ***METRO BANK**

Exhibit 13.7

Perceptual Map: The Bank That Best Satisfies Individual Performance Attributes

*NATIONAL BANK
*SECOND FEDERAL

*Best management

*Best for savings

*Overall satisfaction

*Courteous employees
*FIRST AMERICAN TRUST

*Best for borrowing

*Best service

*METRO BANK

*Community involvement

*SECURITY BANK

Benchmarking

In applying the results of customer satisfaction research, the organization must, once its internal operations have been examined, reach outward to capture external ideas and views. This process is known as *benchmarking* and involves comparisons with recognized industry leaders. Comparisons with the best-performing companies tend to develop an external focus that leads to more challenging goals and objectives. It should be noted that these superior companies are not necessarily competitors.

Benchmarking is centered on identifying the best organizations, documenting the procedures and practices that make them exceptional, and then adopting these outstanding business practices. Information for benchmarking may be found in trade periodicals and professional associations. Also, industry experts and consulting firms can offer advice. The process, however, will ultimately involve a benchmarking partner organization that is willing to share and compare information.

Benchmarking is emphasized in the Malcolm Baldrige requirements:

> Comparison of customer satisfaction results with industry averages, industry leaders, and world leaders.

It compares processes and procedures, not just satisfaction scores. Benchmarking might begin by attacking the performance attributes with the lowest scores. For example, suppose that "negotiating volume discounts" receives a consistently low score. The benchmarking process will discover how the best companies handle the administration of volume discounts.

Literature on competitive benchmarking is relatively scarce. The best current source of information on the subject is Camp's text.

Total Quality Management

Early efforts to achieve quality were focused on product inspection. Over time, statistical quality and process control techniques added sophistication to the inspection process. Employee attitude, motivation, and morale research developed independently of the product inspection process. Marketing research, customer service, and new-product development also expanded without direct links to typical "quality" functions.

The *total quality management* approach unifies the various organizational activities that affect quality. This approach recognizes that important interactions occur among traditional product-quality functions, employee attitudes and motivation, relationships with suppliers, new-product development, and manufacturing. Quality and customer satisfaction are not achieved in isolation.

Customer satisfaction is a major component of the development of a total quality management process. The customer drives the process by establishing the expectations, standards, and requirements. The focus is on adding value to products and services from the customers' perspective. Products and services are viewed as solutions to customer problems. Customer satisfaction research, therefore, is a catalyst in developing a total quality management process.

Customer satisfaction is not just the name of a department or the responsibility of a particular group. The commitment to customer satisfaction must be demonstrated throughout the company and integrated into all phases of the business—product design, production processes, distribution procedures, marketing and sales functions, customer service, billing, and all other functions of the business.

A commitment to customer satisfaction must be incorporated in the company mission statement and in individual job descriptions. The commitment must be apparent when economic conditions are poor as well as when conditions are good.

Quality management requires the active leadership of all members of senior management. Recognition and reward systems are also crucial. An emphasis on continuous improvement in quality and customer satisfaction is always characteristic of the process.

The total quality management approach recognizes that statistical control and inspection procedures are the major means of ensuring quality. Total quality management, however, views quality as a competitive weapon and not just an inspection function. Quality is not defined by internal specifications and control charts. Quality and customer satisfaction are defined by the customers as they compare the capabilities of companies and competitors.

Implementation of total quality management is becoming a requirement rather than an option for some companies. Larger companies are demanding that suppliers implement the total quality management process to ensure a continued business relationship.

The literature on the implementation of the quality management philosophy has increased dramatically in the past few years. Garvin offers excellent insight into the total quality management process. Sixteen essays about quality management, written by executives of leading companies, are presented in Caroprese's text.

The following case study illustrates the implementation of customer satisfaction research results by a firm that has adopted the total quality management approach.

CASE STUDY

Implementing Customer Satisfaction at Roadway Express

Roadway Express moves freight across the continental United States using a distribution network consisting of neighborhood terminals, consolidation hub facilities, and driver relay operations. Roadway also serves Canada, Mexico, Alaska, Hawaii, Puerto Rico, Guam, and more than 20 countries in Europe. This international system utilizes more than 26,000 employees in over 680 freight terminals and offices.

Roadway Express's primary service is transporting long-haul, less-than-truckload freight. Long-haul freight generally comprises shipments traveling in excess of 500 miles. The less-than-truckload operation involves efficiently combining freight from several customers going to one geographic destination.

Satellite terminals across the country pick up freight each day from local customers. This freight is moved during the night to hub centers, where it is consolidated with shipments picked up by other satellites. The consolidations create full trailer loads. These loads are then moved to a hub serving the terminals in the destination area.

Freight transported between hub facilities is moved through relays similar to the old Pony Express system. Upon reaching the destination hub, freight is distributed to satellite terminals for delivery to customers.

Competition intensified greatly with the deregulation of the transportation industry in 1980. Satisfying customer expectations and requirements became a major priority of the long-haul, less-than-truckload carriers.

Roadway Express began formal customer satisfaction research in 1988. The base for the research was Roadway's 50 years of experience in the business combined with relevant studies conducted by a major university. Using these sources as a frame of reference, Roadway Express undertook extensive research with the goal of understanding customer satisfaction and quality service from the customer's perspective.

The objective was to develop a framework for tracking customer satisfaction, carrier performance, and service opportunities on a continuous basis. Telephone interviews were conducted with 1,000 randomly selected users of long-haul, less-than-truckload services. The sample was stratified by customer size and geographic region. The customers included both users and nonusers of Roadway Express.

To explain the purpose of the research and to solicit cooperation, respondents were first contacted by mail. A telephone call was then made to schedule a convenient time for the interview. The length of the interview was approximately 25 minutes.

The interview centered on 31 key service attributes. Customers expressed opinions about both the importance of each attribute and whether their requirements relative to the attribute were being satisfied.

Factor analysis indicated that the 31 service attributes could be summarized in 5 statistically significant dimensions: capabilities to perform the service, competitive pricing, interactions between the customer and the transportation supplier, transit times, and a general comfort level with the transportation company.

Executive judgment and statistical techniques were used to select two or three service attributes from each dimension. These service attributes became the base for a quarterly customer satisfaction survey. The quarterly survey is concerned with the ratings of Roadway Express and several competitors with respect to overall service and performance relative to each specific service attribute.

Several enhancements have been added as the quarterly survey has evolved. Open-ended questions are included to capture the specific reasons why customers rate Roadway Express low with respect to service attributes. Another question deals with why customers have increased or decreased their business with Roadway Express.

Information is segmented by customer account size, geographic region, and type of industry. Customer satisfaction studies are also conducted within selected target industries. The basic satisfaction

continued

questionnaire has been modified to capture service and competitive information specific to each particular industry.

The results of the quarterly customer satisfaction surveys are promptly distributed to all Roadway Express facilities. Company-wide, regional, and local performance is compared and contrasted.

Roadway Express's compensation system is directly correlated with performance and goal attainment. Customer satisfaction is a major component in determining compensation. The system is implemented in a decentralized manner so that improvements at a local level directly affect compensation.

Roadway Express also correlates customer satisfaction information with other measures of performance: billing adjustments, damage claims, late-delivery statistics, missed pickup and delivery appointments, and safety performance.

Rich Vignos, Director of Marketing Research and Development, says of Roadway Express's experiences with customer satisfaction research:

> This ongoing research has been very instrumental in raising the consciousness of our employees about the concept of customer satisfaction and focusing their attention on the importance of specific elements of our service. In addition, the research has also provided Roadway Express management with a significant amount of strategic information that has been utilized in our planning process.
>
> Roadway Express has adopted the Total Quality Management (TQM) structure as its framework for running our business. As a result, the measurement of customer satisfaction will continue to be a priority at Roadway Express and the survey findings will be a key element in the company's continuous improvement efforts.

14

Maintaining Customer Satisfaction

Continuous Improvement Is Not a Luxury

C ontinuous improvement is the secret to maintaining customer satisfaction. Clear, consistent, and systematic improvement is necessary to demonstrate that customer satisfaction is a strategic business objective and not another short-term program. Employees, executives, and customers have all too frequently been subjected to excitement and hype that eventually faded with no lasting effect. Improving customer satisfaction must be a long-term business priority.

Customer satisfaction research demonstrates the need for continuous improvement. About 30 percent of a typical company's customers give the highest scores to three key measures of satisfaction: the overall rating, anticipated future use, and willingness to recommend the company to others. Seven customers out of ten still see room for improvement.

Both the underlying performance attributes and company performance must be periodically monitored. Customer satisfaction is a moving target. Customer expectations and performance standards are continually changing, because the competition is also working to meet or exceed customer requirements. Ongoing focus groups should address how customers view improvements and what remains to be accomplished.

Different surveys, depending on customer characteristics, can be used to emphasize different aspects of customer satisfaction. A transaction-based survey, for example, might be more appropriate for a new customer, whereas an image-based survey may be more applicable for an established customer.

Employee participation should be reinforced with continued training and management by example. Feedback of ongoing research results, implementation of improvements, and areas where additional progress is still desired should be communicated to employees on a periodic basis.

Continuous Improvement

The idea of continuously improving a product or service is not ingrained in U.S. business. The celebrated success of U.S. industry following World War II contributed to executive complacency. Striving for perfection was not a high priority when America led the world in quality and productivity. Continuous improvement was not considered an economically viable strategy. The laws of diminishing returns seemed to indicate that the costs to achieve perfection were not worth the additional investment.

Statistical techniques based on acceptable levels of defects and the probabilities of accepting poor quality were the cornerstone of Japanese industrial progress over the past four decades.

Statistics can add realism to continuous improvement goals and objectives. Suppose, for example, that a management objective is to increase overall satisfaction from a current level of 4.235 to a projected level of 4.500. Statistical techniques can offer guidance in determining the ease or difficulty of achieving this objective.

Statistical techniques, however, received misguided emphasis for several decades, and, indeed, have been severely criticized in recent years. Production control, for example, focused on measuring conformance to an established standard rather than on improving a process. Acceptable levels of defects evolved from a useful statistical quality control concept to a misdirected management philosophy for establishing quality standards.

Statistical techniques are important tools to measure conformance to standards. The tools, however, should not be used in isolation to formulate performance standards. Customer requirements, not statistical theory, must be the guiding force in establishing performance standards.

Business remained successful while the rest of the world played catch-up with U.S. industry. The catch-up ended in the 1980s as U.S. standards for quality and customer satisfaction were surpassed by foreign competitors.

The following case study presents an excellent illustration of how continuous improvement can be implemented by combining a strong management commitment with research, training, and technology.

C A S E   S T U D Y

The National Survey Research Center

The National Survey Research Center initiated a quarterly research project with a client firm in 1970. The research has continued for over two decades. The current methodology for conducting interviews, however, bears little resemblance to the procedures used two decades ago.

The survey has always been conducted using telephone interviews. Twenty years ago the interviewers used paper and pencil and made the telephone calls from their own homes. The complex questionnaire involves over 30 possible branches. Mistakes in the branching patterns were inevitable because of the survey complexity and lack of direct supervision.

continued

The editing process uncovered many of the errors. Respondents were called back to obtain the required information. This added cost to the research and created an unstructured environment where interviews were not conducted in exactly the same manner. Some branching errors remained even after editing, and an error rate of 2 percent to 3 percent was considered acceptable.

A centralized telephone interviewing facility provided the opportunity for direct supervision of interviewers. Implementation of computer-assisted interviewing technology eliminated all branching errors. The acceptable error rate was reduced to zero. Although this was an outstanding improvement, the computer technology offered even more advantages.

Consistency checks were added to investigate possible respondent errors. For example, suppose that a heating system in a home is said to be 15 years old, and that later the interviewer determines that the home is only 10 years old. Since used heating systems are rarely installed in homes, the interviewer receives instructions to clarify the apparent problem and to correct any inaccurate information.

The elimination of branching and logical errors led to the addition of new questions that required even more complex branching logic. Certain combinations of responses triggered different sequences of questions. This provided additional in-depth insight that had not been possible until the computer technology was implemented.

After the mechanical aspects of improving the survey had been fully implemented, emphasis shifted to improving the probing of open-ended responses. Concentration in this area was possible since the time-consuming process of editing and correcting manual questionnaires had been eliminated.

Implementation of computer-assisted interviewing enabled the National Survey Research Center to provide a vastly improved product to its client. Client expectations were thus raised and fulfilled at each stage.

Exceeding Customer Expectations

Continuous improvement implies that business philosophies must change from *meeting* expectations to *exceeding* expectations. Exceeding customer expectations is a challenging goal, because customers continually revise and upgrade their expectations.

Earlier in this book, the advice was given not to combine "excellent" and "very good" ratings because the combined score may not be sensitive to shifts between the two categories. Continuous improvement offers an even better reason for not combining the two ratings: Very good is not good enough if the goal is to *exceed* customer expectations.

The steps necessary to implement an organized process for exceeding expectations are:

1. Define the critical performance attributes that influence how customers choose products, services, and companies.

2. Determine the performance standards and expectations associated with these attributes.

3. Quantify the performance of the company and its major competitors in satisfying these expectations.

4. *Implement Priority* 1: Excel at satisfying the performance attributes and expectations that influence how customers choose products, services, and companies.

5. Determine the performance attributes that create customer satisfaction after the choice of products, services, and companies has been made.

6. Quantify the performance of the company and its major competitors in satisfying this set of performance attributes.

7. *Implement Priority* 2: Excel at satisfying the performance attributes and expectations that satisfy customers after they have selected a product or service.

8. Classify the performance attributes into basic factors, performance factors, and excitement factors.

9. Quantify the performance of the company and its major competitors in satisfying the excitement factors.

10. *Implement Priority* 3: Emphasize satisfying and exceeding both the performance and the excitement factors.

Priority 1 strategies are geared to cultivating new customers. Priority 2 strategies are designed to satisfy current customers. Priority 3 strategies are aimed at building customer loyalty.

Customer and Supplier Business Partnerships

A partnership between supplier and customer is inherent in the total quality management process. The performance attributes that tend to be most important in business partnerships include product quality, delivery time, availability, service, responsiveness, inventory and other cost control measures, technology, and price.

How customers perceive companies that have implemented this approach is indicated by the following customer comments:

> They have joined with our company as a partnership. They have made a commitment to us and they keep the commitment even if they have to do extra work.

> They are more innovative in the way they do business. They are willing to sacrifice to satisfy a particular need that I have.

> They steer me to what is best for me even if it isn't always best for them. They understand us rather than trying to get us to meet their standards of doing business.

> They know the requirements of this company. They bend over backwards to please us.

> When they see they can save us money, they call us to talk about it. That's great!

> I just got this job. They are helping me learn about different aspects of the job that I should know about. I call a lot and they never get mad. Sometimes I repeat myself and they are still nice to me. They even call me on their own to check. Some companies call and just want your business. They work with me. It's teamwork.

> They look at us as a customer for years to come as opposed to just getting through the next year.

A successful business partnership produces tangible results and rewards for both companies. They may involve developing common goals, sharing technology, or participating in customer/client quality teams. Some companies are asking customers to complete performance evaluations on sales representatives.

The growth of business partnerships will reduce the total number of vendors supplying products or services to a company. The suppliers who understand the expectations and requirements of their customers will be in the envious position of receiving even more business as the number of vendors decreases.

The Commitment to Customer Satisfaction

Customer satisfaction research is neither quick nor easy. Six months elapsed time from developing a request for a proposal to receiving the first customer satisfaction ratings is not uncommon. A significant commitment of company personnel is necessary, even if an outside research company manages the interviewing and analysis phases.

Research is only the beginning of the process dedicated to improving customer satisfaction. The research generates among customers an expectation for improvement that must be satisfied. An effort of this magnitude should be undertaken only if management's desire to learn is strong and its commitment to making changes is substantial.

The results, however, are invariably worth the effort. Here are examples of how customers view the importance of service and satisfaction:

The ball is in their court. If they do right by me, they can have my business.

We are happy with the way they do business, so we give them more business.

They think they will be around when everyone else is gone, when in fact the other companies are going to put them out of business with customer service.

They like to tell me how good they are but a competitor came in and showed me how good they were.

They want the business but they can't give us the service.

Customers place a high degree of importance on general business policies and practices. Interpersonal relationships, for example, are almost always important:

> I like the sales rep and I deal with him a lot. It's more of a friend type relationship. I like that.

> I like to deal with a person, not just a company. As a result, I give more business to another company that gives us more personal attention.

Customers expect that a product or service will satisfy a need and will not create problems:

> We have no problems with them, so we are using them more.

> I haven't had any service problems and as long as they continue to meet my needs, I will stay with them.

> I just cannot forget that they just wouldn't take care of a certain problem. I tell my friends not to buy from them either.

> It does us no good to be in business if all we are doing is correcting their mistakes.

Just as many dissatisfied customers do not register formal complaints, satisfied customers may not provide the feedback necessary to understand why satisfaction has occurred. Customer satisfaction research must actively solicit the opinions and comments of customers. Important perspectives will not be obtained without formal research. For example:

> They are a big company and they act like a mom and pop company. They have a smile and they go the extra mile.

> It used to be a pretty shabby company, but the people there today are really aspiring to excellence.

> A long time ago they used to have the image of intimacy and caring. Now they are just another corporation—just another big business.

I think they lied to us when they got our account—how they were going to look after us. Once they had us as a customer, they didn't care about us at all.

My complaints just seem to be falling on deaf ears. I know there are other companies that will give us the service we want.

They really show a lack of interest in our business but plenty of other companies would love to get our business.

Satisfied customers are absolutely vital to business success. Competitive pressures, already intense, are likely to increase in the future. Customer satisfaction research generates knowledge that is critical to a company's obtaining and keeping the competitive advantage.

Appendix

Malcolm Baldrige National Quality Award

Customer Satisfaction Components

Knowledge of Customer Requirements and Expectations—50 Points

- Process for identifying market segments, customer and potential customer groups, including customers of competitors and their requirements and expectations, through surveys, interviews, and other contacts

- Process for identifying product and service quality features and the relative importance of these features to customers or customer groups

- Cross-comparisons with other key data and information such as complaints, losses, and gains of customers, and performance data that may yield information on customer requirements and expectations and on key product and service features

- How the company evaluates and improves the effectiveness of its processes for determining customer requirements and expectations, such as improved surveys, other customer contacts, analysis, or cross-comparisons

Customer Relationship Management—30 Points

- Process for ensuring that customer service requirements are understood and responded to throughout the company

- Means for ensuring easy access for customers to comment, seek assistance, and complain

- Follow-up with customers on products and services to determine satisfaction and to gain information for improvement

- Empowering customer-contact employees to resolve problems promptly and to take extraordinary measures when appropriate

- Special hiring requirements, attitudinal and other training, recognition and attitude/morale determination of customer-contact employees

- Technology and logistics support to enable customer-contact employees to provide effective and timely customer service

- Analysis of complaint information, gains and losses of customers, and lost orders to assess costs and market consequences for policy review

- Process for evaluating and improving services to customers

Customer Service Standards—20 Points

- Selection of well-defined, objectively measurable standards derived from customer requirements and expectations

- Employee involvement in developing, evaluating, and improving or changing standards

- Deployment of requirements and/or standards information to all company units to ensure effective support for customer-contact employees who are expected to meet the company's customer-service standards

- Tracking to ensure that key service standards are met

- How service standards are evaluated and improved

Commitment to Customers—20 Points

- Product and service guarantees and product warranties: comprehensiveness, conditions, understandability, and credibility

- Other types of commitments the company makes to promote trust and confidence in its products and/or services

- How improvements in the company's products and/or services over the past three years have been translated into changes in guarantees, warranties, and other commitments

Complaint Resolution for Quality Improvement—30 Points

- Process for ensuring that formal and informal complaints and critical comments made to different company units are aggregated for overall evaluation and use wherever appropriate throughout the company

- Process for ensuring that complaints are resolved promptly by customer-contact employees

- Summarize indicators of improved response including trends in response time

- Process for analyzing complaints to determine underlying causes and using this information to make improvements such as in processes, standards, and information to customers

- Process for evaluating the company's handling of complaints to improve both the response to complaints and the ability to translate the findings into preventative measures

Customer Satisfaction Determination—50 Points

- Types and frequency of methods used, including procedures to ensure objectivity and validity

- How satisfaction is segmented by customer groups, if appropriate, and how satisfaction relative to competitors is determined

- Correlation of satisfaction results with other satisfaction indicators such as complaints and gains and losses of customers

- How information on key products and service quality features that determine customer preference is extracted from customer satisfaction data

- How customer satisfaction information is used in quality improvement

- Process used to evaluate and improve methods for determining customer satisfaction

Customer Satisfaction Results—50 Points

- Trends in customer satisfaction and key customer satisfaction indicators for products and services segmented by customer groups, if appropriate

- Trends in major adverse indicators such as complaints, claims, refunds, mandatory recalls, returns, repeat services, replacements, downgrades, repairs, warranty costs, and warranty work

Customer Satisfaction Comparisons—50 Points

- Comparison of customer satisfaction results with industry averages, industry leaders, and world leaders, or with other competitors in the company's key markets

- Surveys, competitive awards, recognition, and ratings by independent organizations, including customers

- Trends in gaining or losing customers

- Trends in gaining or losing market share relative to major competitors, domestic and foreign

Bibliography

Bogdan, R., and S. T. Taylor, *Introduction to Qualitative Research*, New York: Wiley, 1975.

Bolfing, C P., and R. B. Woodruff, "Effects of Situational Involvement on Consumers' Use of Standards in Satisfaction/Dissatisfaction Processes," *Journal of Consumer Satisfaction, Dissatisfaction and Complaining Behavior*, Vol. 1, 1988.

Brandt, D. R., "How Service Marketers Can Identify Value-Enhancing Service Elements," *Journal of Services Marketing* 2, no. 3 (Summer, 1988).

Camp, R. C., *Benchmarking*, Milwaukee: Quality Press, 1989.

Cardozo, R. N., "Customer Satisfaction: Laboratory Study and Marketing Action," in L. G. Smith, ed., *Reflections on Progress in Marketing*, Chicago: American Marketing Association, 1964.

Carley, K., "Formalizing the Social Expert's Knowledge," *Sociological Methods and Research*, 17, no. 2 (November 1988).

Caroprese, F., *Making Total Quality Happen*, New York: Conference Board, 1990.

Churchill, G. A., and C. Suprenant, "An Investigation into the Determinants of Customer Satisfaction," *Journal of Marketing Research*, 19 (November 1982).

Converse, J. M., and S. Presser, *Survey Questions*, Beverly Hills, CA: Sage Publications, 1986.

219

Cooley, W. W., and P. R. Lohnes, *Multivariate Data Analysis,* New York: Wiley, 1971.

Crosby, P. B., *Quality Is Free,* New York: New American Library, 1979.

DeMaio, T. J., "Refusals: Who, Where and Why," *Public Opinion Quarterly,* Summer 1980.

Deming, W. E., *Sample Design in Business Research,* New York: John Wiley and Sons, 1960.

Desatnick, R. L., "Managing to Keep the Customer," San Francisco: Jossey-Bass, 1987.

Dillman, D. A., "Mail and Telephone Surveys: The Total Design Method," New York: Wiley, 1978.

Draper, N. R., and H. Smith, "Applied Regression Analysis," New York: Wiley, 1967.

Erdos, P. L., *Professional Mail Surveys,* Huntington, NY: R. E. Krieger Publishing, 1983.

Erevelles, S., and C. Leavitt, "A Comparison of Current Models of Consumer Satisfaction/Dissatisfaction," *Journal of Consumer Satisfaction, Dissatisfaction and Complaining Behavior,* 5 (1992).

Frey, J. H., *Survey Research by Telephone,* Beverly Hills, CA: Sage Publications, 1983.

Fuller, C. H., "Weighting to Adjust for Survey Nonresponse," *Public Opinion Quarterly,* Summer 1974.

Garvin, D. A., "Managing Quality," New York: Free Press, 1988.

Geer, J. G., "What Do Open-Ended Questions Measure?" *Public Opinion Quarterly,* 52 (1988): 365–371.

Geer, J. G., "Do Open-Ended Questions Measure Salient Issues?" *Public Opinion Quarterly,* Fall 1991.

Gilly, M. C., "Postcomplaint Processes: From Organizational Response to Repurchase Behavior," *Journal of Consumer Affairs* 21 (1987).

Goodstadt, M. S., L. Chung, R. Kronitz, and G. Cook, "Mail Survey Response Rates: Their Manipulation and Impact," *Journal of Marketing Research,* August 1977.

Grant, E. L., and R. S. Leavenworth, *Statistical Quality Control,* 5th ed., New York: McGraw-Hill, 1980.

Halstead, D., and T. J. Page, "The Effects of Satisfaction and Complaining Behavior on Consumer Repurchase Intentions," *Journal of Customer Satisfaction, Dissatisfaction and Complaining Behavior,* 5 (1992).

Hanna, M., and P. Karp, *Customer Satisfaction,* New York: American Management Association, 1989.

Henry, G. T., *Practical Sampling,* Newbury Park, CA: Sage Publications, 1990.

Hensley, W. E., "Increasing Response Rate by Choice of Postage Stamps," *Public Opinion Quarterly,* Summer 1974.

Hoffman, D. L., and G. R. Franke, "Correspondence Analysis: Graphical Representation of Categorical Data in Marketing Research," *Journal of Marketing Research,* August 1986.

Hughes, M. A., and D. E. Garrett, "Intercoder Reliability Estimation Approaches in Marketing: A Generalizability Theory Framework," *Journal of Marketing Research,* May 1990.

Hunt, S. D., R. D. Sparkman, Jr., and J. B. Wilcox, "The Pretest in Survey Research: Issues and Preliminary Findings," *Journal of Marketing Research* 19 (1982).

Jacoby, J., and J. J. Jaccard, "The Sources, Meaning and Validity of Consumer Complaint Behavior: A Psychological Analysis," *Journal of Retailing,* 57 (1981).

Jordan, B., and L. Suchman, "Interactional Troubles in Survey Interviews," *Proceedings of the American Statistical Association, Survey Research Methods,* 1987.

Juran, J. M., *Juran on Leadership for Quality,* New York: Free Press, 1989.

Juran, J. M., *Juran on Planning for Quality,* New York: Free Press, 1988.

Kalton, G., and R. Stowell, "A Study of Coder Variability," *Applied Statistics* 28 (1979).

Kish, L., *Survey Sampling,* New York: John Wiley and Sons, 1965.

Klecka, W. R., *Discriminant Analysis,* Beverly Hills, CA: Sage Publications, 1980.

Krueger, R. A., *Focus Groups: A Practical Guide for Applied Research,* Beverly Hills, CA: Sage Publications.

Lavrakas, P. J., *Telephone Survey Methods,* Beverly Hills, CA: Sage Publications.

Lele, M. M., *The Customer Is Key,* New York: Wiley, 1987.

Liswood, L. A., *Serving Them Right,* New York: Harper Business, 1990.

Mandell, L., "When to Weight: Determining Nonresponse Bias in Survey Data," *Public Opinion Quarterly,* Summer 1974.

Marr, J. W., "Letting the Customer Be the Judge of Quality," *Quality Progress,* 1986.

Payne, S. L., "The Art of Asking Questions," Princeton, N.J.: Princeton University Press, 1951.

Peters, T. L., *Thriving on Chaos,* New York: Knopf, 1988.

Peters, T. L., and R. H. Waterman, Jr., *In Search of Excellence,* New York: Harper and Row, 1982.

Richins, M. L., and P. H. Bloch, "The Role of Situational and Enduring Involvement in Post-Purchase Product Evaluation," *Journal of Consumer Satisfaction, Dissatisfaction and Complaining Behavior,* Vol. 1, 1988.

Rummel, R. J., *Applied Factor Analysis,* Evanston, IL: Northwestern University Press, 1970.

Schuman, H., and S. Presser, "The Open and Closed Question," *American Sociological Review* 44 (1979).

Spector, P. E., *Summated Rating Scale Constructing*, Beverly Hills, CA: Sage Publications, 1992.

Spreng, R. A., and R. W. Olshavsky, "A Desires-as-Standard Model of Customer Satisfaction: Implications for Measuring Satisfaction," *Journal of Satisfaction, Dissatisfaction and Complaining Behavior* 5 (1992).

Sudman, S., *Response Effect in Surveys*, Chicago: Aldine Publishing, 1974.

TARP, (Technical Assistance Research Program), *Consumer Complaint Handling in America: An Update Study*, White House Office of Consumer Affairs, 1979.

Tuckel, P. S., and B. M. Feinberg, "The Answering Machine Poses Many Questions for Telephone Survey Researchers," *Public Opinion Quarterly*, Summer 1991.

Urban, G., and J. Hauser, *Design and Marketing of New Products*, Englewood Cliffs, N.J.: Prentice-Hall, 1980.

Weber, R. P., *Basic Content Analysis*, Beverly Hills, CA. Sage Publications, 1990.

Weller, S. C., and A. K. Romney, *Metric Scaling*, Beverly Hills, CA: Sage Publications, 1990.

Wiseman, F., and P. McDonald, "Toward the Development of Industry Standards for Response and Nonresponse Rates," Report No. 80-101, Cambridge, MA: Marketing Science Institute, 1980.

Woodruff, R. B., E. R. Cadotte, and R. L. Jenkins, "Modeling Consumer Satisfaction Processes Using Experience-Based Norms," *Journal of Marketing Research*, 20 (August 1983).

Woodruff, R. B., D. S. Clemons, D. W. Schumann, S. F. Gardial, and M. J. Burns, "The Standards Issue in Customer Satisfaction/Dissatisfaction Research: A Historical Perspective," *Journal of Consumer Satisfaction, Dissatisfaction and Complaining Behavior* 4 (1991).

Index

American Marketing Association

YOU NEVER GET ENOUGH...
As a marketing professional you'll never get enough information about marketing. The body of knowledge is being added to constantly. Success stories, and even stories of failure, are written daily.

There's only one way to stay up-to-date with the latest academic theories, the "war" stories, the global techniques, and the leading technologies.

Become a member of the American Marketing Association.

For a free membership information kit;
call us at 312-648-0536
FAX us at 312-993-7542
write us at 250 S. Wacker Drive, Chicago, Illinois 60606
or contact your local AMA chapter.